HOW TO WRITE A
TRULY
GREAT
NOVEL
The Writers' Desk Book

Lindsay Grier Arthur

ARCHWAY
PUBLISHING

Archway Publishing books may be ordered
through booksellers or by contacting:

Archway Publishing
1663 Liberty Drive
Bloomington, IN 47403
www.archwaypublishing.com
1 (888) 242-5904

ISBN: 978-1-4808-6671-3 (sc)
ISBN: 978-1-4808-6672-0 (e)

Library of Congress Control Number: 2018909225

Print information available on the last page.

Archway Publishing rev. date: 08/27/2018

CONTENTS

PART THREE
Finishing Touches

INTRODUCTION

Anyone with a reasonable command of the English language is capable of writing good fiction. This book provides everyone who has dreamed of writing a novel or other creative work with the tools needed to realize that dream. It is conveniently organized to serve both as an instructional guide to improve the creative writing skills of first-time authors as well as a desk book to assist all writers in planning, writing, and editing any creative writing project.

While I speak with the voice of a published author, both fiction and non-fiction, more importantly I speak with the voice of a teacher and writing coach. Not all good writers are good teachers, because often all they know is what works for them. As both a teacher of creative writing and a published author, I have a unique and fresh perspective on the art of writing fiction. As an author, I enjoy writing well; as a teacher, I enjoy showing others how to write well.

The hallmark of all good fiction is to create a captivating story populated with compelling characters. The goal of this book is to provide a clear and concise roadmap that assists writers to achieve this objective, a roadmap that is easily understood and easily applied both by novice writers and by seasoned writers who strive to improve their manuscripts.

The best way to understand how to write great fiction is to start by examining what I call The Seven Principles of Literary Excellence. Here's my list.

1. **Compelling Characters** is an essential component of all good fiction as well as a primary driver of reader engagement.
2. **A Captivating Story** is an essential component of all good fiction as well as a prime force in creating an enjoyable experience for the reader.
3. **Conflict** is essential in building both compelling characters and captivating stories.
4. **Emotion** is a prime driver of character development.
5. **Mystery and Suspense** are prime drivers of a captivating story.
6. **Artistic Vision** is the lens through which the reader becomes emotionally attached to, or repulsed by, the main characters.
7. **Showing not telling** is an essential tool that brings the reader into the heat of the action to experience the story first hand as it unfolds.

Once these principles are understood, the second step is to learn how to apply the many tools available to writers to develop compelling characters and captivating stories. My focus is on what I consider to be the six most important tools to master. Here's my list.

1. **Pre-writing organization**: the storyboard, the scene chart, character profiles, and chapter outlines.
2. The use of **emotive verbs** to develop compelling characters and powerful stories.
3. The use of **similes, metaphors, and side scenes** to create compelling characters.
4. The proper way to use of **dialogue** to create compelling characters.
5. The **all-important first page**.
6. The best **point of view**, that is, who is most suited to tell the story.

I divide the book into three parts. In Part One, I cover the seven principles of literary excellence. Each principle is the subject of a separate chapter, and every chapter contains not only a clear explanation of what is required but also numerous examples that illustrate how to apply the principle successfully. Each chapter also contains a writing drill designed to force students, in a brief writing exercise, to apply the principle that is the subject of the chapter. My own suggestions for completing the drills are included at the end of the book.

Part Two focuses on the most important techniques that good writers employ to develop compelling characters, the heart of all fiction writing, and to write stories that captivate, engross, and arouse readers. I begin Part Two with a discussion of how successful writers plan a great plot that will drive the characters and enchant the readers. I offer clear step-by-step suggestions for using dialogue, similes, metaphors, side scenes and verb selection to build characters. Finally, I discuss the pros and cons associated with a writer's choice of narrator.

Part Three is clean up. It addresses proven editing techniques, avoiding and overcoming writers' block, and publishing options.

It took me eight drafts to get my novel to a level where it could be published. I made a lot of mistakes and wasted an enormous amount of time fixing them. My hope is that all my students and all readers of this book can avoid the stress and wasted time that I experienced and produce a top-quality manuscript in only two drafts. And, most of all, I want all budding writers to experience the grand exhilaration that comes from feeling the creative juices erupt onto the page to produce a manuscript that gives them enormous pride and satisfaction. The goal of this book is to make writing fun, stimulating and satisfying by eliminating the stress and self-doubt that can destroy the creative experience.

Part One

Seven Principles of Literary Excellence And How to Use them

CHAPTER 1

Conflict and Tension

Literary conflict is essential in building compelling characters and captivating stories.

C onflict plays an essential role in all great works of fiction. Without conflict, stories are bland, characters are flat, and readers are bored. It's often correctly observed that if the characters are happy, the reader is not. This literary paradox results from the fact that while virtually everyone strives to avoid conflict and tension in our own lives, we are nevertheless enthralled to read about it in our novels. We love to watch little people with big dreams struggle mightily against seemingly insurmountable hurdles. We love to watch everyday people struggle to overcome racial, gender, and ethnic discrimination, to see the poor and weak fight hopeless battles against the rich and strong, to watch people struggle to survive in the face of natural disasters or cataclysmic events, to see people battle to overcome their own physical disabilities and character flaws, to see people fight against social injustice and abusive political power, and we love to see enemies struggle to find love.

Let me state my case as forcefully as I can -- there are very few great works of fiction where the main characters do not face enormous hurdles to achieve monumental goals. Without conflict there is no story at all, at least not an interesting one. As writers, we must be merciless in making trouble for our characters. The more the character is challenged, the more he must reveal himself. The longer the challenge exists, the more the reader bonds with the character and enmeshes himself in his story. Only through conflict can the reader fully engage the character, for better or for worse.

I consider the terms "conflict" and "tension" to be essentially synonymous although they have slightly different connotations. Conflict is the challenge main characters must resolve in order to achieve their goals. Tension is literally a pulling apart, in other words, an internal stress. Thus "conflict" seems to be the better word to describe external conflicts (e.g. conflicting goals between two people) whereas "tension" may more accurately describe internal conflicts (e.g., overcoming disabilities and character flaws). Use whatever word feels more comfortable to you, but in this book, I use the word "conflict" more often because I think it's easier to understand in a literary context.

There are two aspects to a character's wants, and both must be present for the character to fully develop. First, the want must be enormously important to the character -- life threatening, life altering, politically or legally epic, ethically or morally impactful to societal norms. Anything less does not distinguish the character from the masses of mere mortals dealing with our everyday hurdles and as such does not allow the character to achieve greatness. Second, the want must be urgent, not the dreams of a child for future fame and fortune. The more urgent the want is; the more the reader is aroused.

Just as the character's wants must be enormous and urgent, so also must the obstacles he faces be of at least equal power and intensity. A character with epic desires cannot achieve greatness if his path to success is easy.

For some reason my students have more difficulty

understanding the proper role of conflict in literature than any of the other seven principles I teach. I've tried presenting the concept using several different techniques, and the one that seems to work best is to explain it in terms of algebraic formulas. Here's the first one, a basic formula for conflict.

Conflict = Want + Obstacles

If one removes either want or obstacle from the mix, then obviously there is no conflict by definition. But not any old want or any old obstacle will work. To fully appreciate the type of conflict that does work, let's start by examining two simple examples of conflict that quite obviously are inadequate.

Example 1

Tom's Want: It would really be nice if I could finish the 10K race next Saturday.
Tom's Obstacle: Pressures at work make training difficult.

Example 2

Mary's Want: Mary wants to make her high school golf team.
Mary's Obstacle: Mary faces strong competition from last year's returning players.

These examples meet the literal definition of conflict; Tom wants to finish a race, but he has little time to train; Mary wants a spot on the team but other players vying for the same spot stand in her way. Conflict, yes, but great story, no. To turn these examples into great stories with interesting characters, we need to ratchet up the level of conflict several notches.

Most authors of How-to-Write Fiction books speak about the need for major conflict. I join their chorus with full lungs a blare.

But, to emphasize the point I go one step further. I assign the concept an enhanced name -- what I like to call Literary Conflict. Here is my formula for Literary Conflict.

Literary Conflict = Major Want + Major Obstacle

Let's see what happens to the examples above when we raise the level of both the wants and the obstacles.

Example 3

Jane's Want: I'm going to make the Olympic track team as a long-distance runner.
Jane's Obstacles: A severe auto accident killed her entire family and left her with a deformed leg, atrophied leg muscles, severe chronic leg pain, and enormous debt that forces her to work extra hours just to keep afloat financially.

Example 4

Mike's Want: Mike wants to win the United States Amateur golf championship.
Mike's Obstacles: Mike's mother is terminally ill and Mike must spend most of his time looking after her; his dad's business goes bankrupt and he can no longer support Mike's golf expenses; his college coach cuts Mike from the team for missing practice after taking his mother to a doctor's appointment; Mike's car dies so he has no transportation to travel to amateur golf tournaments; Mike's golf clubs are stolen and he has to play with an old set he had as a teenager; Mike sustains a low back injury when he is hit by a drunk driver riding his bicycle to the golf practice range.

Are you with me? Who are the more compelling characters, Tom or Jane? Mary or Mike? Which of the stories would you find more captivating as a reader? The only difference between these stories is the enormity of the wants and obstacles.

I rest my case. Nobody cares much about poor Tom because he is not doing anything extraordinary. On the other hand, every reader will fall in love with Jane. They will feel her pain as their own. They will be on the sidelines cheering her on, praying for her, crying as she endures setbacks, leaping for joy when she moves a step closer, and calling all their friends to read her story when Jane finally makes the Olympic team.

Examples 3 and 4 are paradigms of literary conflict at its best. Jane and Mike have the potential to become extremely compelling and empathetic characters as they struggle toward their challenging and illusive goals, all because the level of conflict they face is dramatically increased. This seems so simple to understand, and my students always nod in unison as I explain the principle of literary conflict in these terms.

But then something goes very wrong. I always give my class a drill that forces them to write a short passage that is consistent with whatever principle we are discussing in class at the time. When I give them the drill on conflict, a drill that requires them to outline a plot with intense conflict, almost invariably I get back a storyline that looks very much like Mary wanting to make the high school golf team. Big deal! Even my more advanced students who are well along on their novels and who have for months been forced to listen to my excoriations about the need for enormous conflict generally deliver manuscripts to me with grossly inadequate conflict. What they write meets the literal definition of "conflict," but it does not meet the enhanced definition of "literary conflict." Their misstep is by far the most common mistake I see in manuscripts of budding writers.

I know exactly why this happens. Most writers, myself included, start with a storyline. This is entirely natural because we writers have generally been mulling over a possible storyline for several years before we actually start writing. We have a great story to tell and, by God, we're going to tell it. The problem is that in planning our storyline, precious little thought is typically given to the important role that conflict plays in our stories, so often at the moment that pen and paper first meet (fingertips and keyboard), serious conflict is missing in action.

This is the wrong way to start writing. Instead of beginning with an interesting storyline, I recommend that writers start by imagining all the conflicts that will drive the story. That may sound a bit mysterious now, but it will all become clear in Chapter 9 – How to Get Started. Don't go there now. Let me instead further clarify my thesis by explaining the essential difference between a "plot" and a "storyline." The difference is easily appreciated by return to my algebraic formulas.

Plot = Literary Conflict + Action + Resolution
Storyline = Action + Resolution

Note that the only difference between these two formulas is the absence of Literary Conflict. A plot has it; a simple storyline does not. Plot is the foundation of the novel, around which the characters and scenes are built. It provides the formal structure through which all events flow in a logical literary sequence. And it is driven by literary conflict. If we remove literary conflict from the right side of the equation, a true plot no longer exists. All that remains is the storyline. Here is my point; when writers initiate works of fiction by focusing on the storyline rather than the plot, they are destined to produce a story with inadequate conflict. Storylines are essential, but they do not a novel make.

One final thought: when I speak of words, my advice is "Less is Better;" when I speak of conflict, my advice is the opposite: "More is Better."

TYPES OF LITERARY CONFLICT

There are many forms of conflict, each of them addressed below. Where the conflict arises by virtue of competing desires between protagonist and antagonist, the ideal approach is to figure out exactly what must happen for the protagonist to succeed and then give the antagonist the power to thwart that route to success. Both sides have comparable urgency and comparable resources. Some of the best novels, however, arise out of conflicts that do not involve any antagonist, for instance, like my examples above about Tom and Jane. So let me expand our understanding of conflict by summarizing the many varied types of conflict available to writers. All of them work well, as long as the basic premises of enormity and urgency are followed.

Person versus person - Protagonist versus Antagonist

1. Conflicting character goals
   The essence of conflict is a clash of wants between two characters, the protagonist and antagonist. The clash must be one that the reader finds interesting. Obvious examples include war stories, sports stories, and stories about epic legal battles.

2. Race and religion
   There have been many outstanding novels based on conflicts associated with race and religion. Some of these also involve conflicting character goals, for instance, when the protagonist and antagonist are from different races or religions. *To Kill a Mockingbird* is a good example.

3. Ethics and morality
   Ethics and morality often serve as the underpinnings
   of great novels. This is particularly true when there is
   a lack of clarity over which character is right, usually
   because the issue is front and center in the public media
   at the time. Examples include abortion, gay and lesbian
   relationships, nuclear weapons, gun control, religious
   freedom, immigration, and the like. Examples include *My
   Sister's Keeper, Never Let Me Go, Crime and Punishment,
   The Plague, The Handmaid's Tale, The Immortal Life of
   Henrietta Lacks*, and *The Citadel*.

4. Altruism versus self-interest
   An example of a conflict between altruism and self-interest
   is a story that explores the American political system and
   whether the public is properly served by a system where
   elected officials primarily promote the self-interests of their
   own constituents rather than the greater public interest of
   the country as a whole. Ayn Rand novels *Atlas Shrugged*
   and *The Fountainhead* immediately come to mind. These
   stories are compelling not merely because they explore the
   role of altruism in American life but because they raise the
   question of whether altruism is even an appropriate value.

5. Social Injustice
   Rich versus poor, strong versus weak, haves versus have-
   nots – each of these and similar issues have produced
   many compelling novels. Often these conflicts are not
   primary but are included as subsidiary conflicts to make
   the protagonist more appealing. Examples include *Oliver
   Twist, Les Miserables, A Christmas Carol, 1984, The Kite
   Runner, The Girl with the Dragon Tatoo, The Boy in the
   Striped Pajamas, The Jungle, Uncle Tom's Cabin, Grapes
   of Wrath*, and *Twelve Years a Slave*.

6. Love between enemies
   Examples include *Romeo-and-Juliet* love stories involving the children of warring families, war stories like *Silent Night* where enemy soldiers ignored orders to fight each other over Christmas, and stories about people overcoming societal proscriptions about associations with classes of people deemed unworthy.

Person versus nature

7. Natural or man-made disasters
   Examples include mine collapse in Chile that trapped 33 miners for 69 days, survival of residents of Hiroshima following dropping of atomic bomb, Haitians' survival following 2010 earthquake, California firemen trapped in a forest fire.

8. Cataclysmic events
   Examples include tsunamis, earthquakes, hurricanes, landslides, and other natural disasters that require one or more characters to struggle enormously just to survive.

9. Adventures
   Examples include Ernest Shackleton's epic voyage to the South Pole, *Wild: From Lost to Found on the Pacific Crest Trail*, Amelia Earhart's flight around the world, Ann Bancroft's artic dogsled expedition.

Person versus self

10. Inner character struggles
    Real people often have trouble addressing their own internal struggles; here are a few examples: fanaticism, superstition, spite, shallowness, myopia, sexuality, numerous phobias, perfectionism, megalomania, lust,

intolerance, illiteracy, hypocrisy, hedonism, egotism and arrogance.

11. Overcoming character flaws
    Internal struggles, for instance, with one's egotism, myopia, racism and bigotry, inability to commit to loving relationship, feelings of inferiority, fear of facing a dysfunctional childhood. Examples include *Little Women, What Made Maddy Run, Those We Love Most*, and *Dancing in the Dark*.

12. Overcoming disabilities, infirmities and hardship
    Examples include *Unbroken, I Am Malala, I Know Why the Caged Bird Sings, The Rosie Project*, biographies about Franklin Roosevelt overcoming polio, biographies about Helen Keller's deafness and blindness, stories about people who have overcome dyslexia, stories about addiction.

Person versus society

13. Person victimized by society
    Examples include Mahatma Gandhi's fight for India's independence, Martin Luther King's fight against racial injustice, stories about the virtual annihilation of the American Indians.

14. Good versus evil
    Examples include *To Kill a Mockingbird, East of Eden, Harry Potter books, The Chronicles of Narnia, The Hobbit, City of Ashes, The school for Good and Evil, City of Fallen Angels, Uncle Tom's Cabin, Roots, The Autobiography of Miss Jane Pitman*, and *A Million Nightingales*.

15. Weak versus strong
    Examples include *The Underground Railroad* and *Rosa*, (the story about Rosa Parks).

16. Politics versus virtue
    Examples include *Macbeth, Darkness at Noon, Chinatown, The Scopes Monkey Trial,* and stories about Joe McCarthy's Anti-American Activities investigations.

Person versus technology

17. Science moving beyond our control
    Steven King science fiction novels

Person versus supernatural

18. Overcoming supernatural threats
    Examples include *The Hunger Games, Harry Potter* books, some Stephen King novels, books about vampires, ghosts, haunted houses, paranormal stories.

One final observation about conflict. The various forms of conflict summarized above are not mutually exclusive. Often the most powerful stories contain multiple forms of conflicts. In laying out one's plot I recommend that that writers consider the complete list and employ as many different forms of conflict as may be appropriate to captivate the reader and create compelling characters.

Chapter 1 Drill

In less than one page, write an outline for a plot you'd really love to read, one that contains intense conflict and a compelling character.

CHAPTER 2

Compelling Characters

> Compelling characters is an essential
> component of all good fiction as well as
> a primary driver of reader engagement.

N o one reads novels to experience the routine humdrum that mostly dominates their own lives. Readers want to meet fascinating, extraordinary people, people who are different from anyone they have ever known. We writers ask our readers to sacrifice a week or more of their time to read our books; what does the reader get in return? Nothing, I say, if he does not enjoy spending his valuable time with the characters we have created.

Call to mind one of your favorite books. What do you remember most about the book, the characters or the plot? This is a rhetorical question, of course, given its standing in a chapter about compelling characters. Readers want to fall in love; they want arousal, to be swept off their feet and be drawn like quicksand into the life of a character that is so fascinating they cannot bear to put the book down.

I once heard a literary instructor say, "There are no new plots; there are only new characters." Unless "plot" is defined very broadly, I would not agree with that assessment, but the point is legitimate – good characters make good novels. The best story with boring characters is a guaranteed failure. A bland story with compelling characters has a much better shot at success. *Tuesdays With Morrie* is a perfect example of a book with a dull storyline made great by a compelling character.

All of this is well known to any seasoned reader of fiction. The real question for this chapter is how does a writer create memorable characters? What tools are available to make characters truly compelling?

The short answer is that there are three primary drivers of character development:

1. Conflict
2. Emotion
3. Artistic Vision

I discuss each of these drivers in detail in Chapters 1, 3, and 6, but I make brief mention of them here because together they are the tools that successful writers employ to create fascinating characters.

CONFLICT.

Conflict is essential. The main characters must push themselves to the limit to achieve their wants, and the obstacles they face must counterattack with equal force. This incites the characters to act, draws them out, and reveals their inner selves and their emotions. More importantly, it draws the reader in. The more pressure that is put on the character, the more he must reveal himself, and the more the reader experiences him and gets tugged into the action. Readers don't like woosies. They are interested in strong characters who want something badly and will do everything, no matter the personal cost, to obtain it.

EMOTION.

The ordeals endured by the main characters give the writer an opportunity to bring out the characters' inner emotions as they strive to realize their dreams. Without emotion, characters become mere automatons rigidly and monotonously wandering through the scenes you create for them. And no reader has any interest in leaping into the life of an automaton.

ARTISTIC VISION.

Both of these words, "artistic" and "vision," are operative. The good writer sees himself not merely as a writer, but as an artist. Great artists paint pictures with oils and acrylics; writers paint pictures with words. What is important here is that readers do not want to see words; they want to see pictures. If you think of yourself exclusively as a writer, you tend to over focus on the words you select when the real focus must be on the images you create. This is the artistic part; now for the vision part.

Human vision is very limited and sees only the outside of people and objects. Readers want to see inside, so you must use superman vision, or Writers' Vision, as I like to say, to take the reader inside your characters. I urge all my students to visit major art museums and study the portraits of the great artists. I urge them to ask themselves why any given portrait has earned its reputation for greatness. Forget about whether you like or dislike the painting; consider only whether the artist has taken you inside the heart and soul of his subject. In the end, that's the true measure of greatness; it is the difference between a snapshot of a woman dressed in black and the Mona Lisa. Here's my thesis: the qualities that make the Mona Lisa a memorable painting are the very same qualities that make any literary character a memorable person. A snap shot of a woman dressed in black does not get inside the woman's heart, which is exactly where our readers want to go.

Let's look at a brief scene I have written to illustrate how conflict, emotion, and artistic vision can be used to build compelling characters. As you read this snippet, focus on each of the three drivers, following which I will ask you to assess my success or failure.

"Mr. Horgan." Sean, a summer intern, barely whispered the name of the bank's Chief Executive Officer as he slipped, unannounced into the spacious corner office.

"How'd you get in here," Horgan demanded.

"Mr. Horgan," Sean repeated, "I need to speak with you about an important matter."

"No one sees me without an appointment. Get out."

"Sir," Sean said, now standing only a few feet from Horgan's grandiose desk. "This is a personal matter."

"Like hell." Horgan picked up the phone and punched a key connecting him to his executive assistant.

"Sir, this is private, quite private really," Sean said. "At least for now."

"Get security up here," Horgan barked into the phone. "Now."

"Sean inched forward to the edge of Charles Horgan's desk, leaned over and quietly said, "This is about Shirley Wayne, sir."

Horgan jumped from his chair, grabbed Sean by his lapels and yelled directly into his face, "Whoever you are, you're fired, get the hell out of my office."

Sean wiped a few speckles of spit from his cheek. "Shirley Wayne is my mother," he said.

Two uniformed men now stood at the doorway and stared into the face of a boiler about to explode. As they waited for instructions that were never issued, Sean eased free of Horgan's grip on his lapel. "Sir," he said, "would tomorrow morning be more convenient for you? I could bring the video with me if you wish."

O.K. what's your verdict? Does this dialogue contain conflict, emotion, and artistic vision? Do Sean and Horgan have the potential to become compelling characters? Let's look.

There is an obvious conflict between the outraged Charles Horgan and Sean. There is also a hint of conflict between the banker and Sean's mother, Shirley Wayne. This conflict is heightened by the disparate positions of the characters, a lowly summer intern and a bank CEO.

The scene also has a nice emotional tone, uncontrolled anger on the part of the banker, and a hint of feistiness and revenge by the intern. Their different emotions are further enhanced by the fact that one would expect each character to have the opposite emotion, composure by the bank CEO and rage by the intern.

Finally, artistic vision is achieved by taking the reader into the states of mind of the two characters. We're shocked by the CEO's overreaction and surprised by the boldness of the intern.

This is a very short dialogue. While compelling characters cannot be constructed in a single scene, the presence in this brief passage of all three factors that drive character development is at least a good beginning. It's easy to imagine how these two characters' continued behaviors will draw the reader into their story, eventually cheering for one and booing at the other.

Note also how this short scene introduces significant mystery and suspense. What did Horgan do to Shirley Wayne? What is captured on the apparent videotape that Sean threatens to produce and make public? Why did the CEO so obviously overreact? Why did the CEO not order security to haul Sean away? Good writers ask these questions, but they do not answer them. There's no point having Sean blurt out the nature of Horgan's perceived transgressions in this first conversation, just as there is no reason to say what's on the videotape. Make the reader wonder, for as long as possible. These little mysteries arouse the reader's curiosity and hook him into the story. More on mystery in Chapter 5.

Let me now spend a few pages describing five additional tools that good writers use to enhance the uniqueness and stature of their characters and make us crazed to learn more about them: exaggeration, physical characteristics, contrast, markers, and ever-fascinating dialogue.

1. Exaggeration.

"Joe was a Paul Bunyan of a man." No one really believes Joe was as big or as strong as Paul Bunyan but the use of the greatly exaggerated metaphor transposes Paul Bunyan's traits onto Joe. Readers will have no trouble picturing Joe as a very large and physically powerful man.

"Woman, I could grow a full beard waiting for you to get dressed." The writer depicts an interesting character trait about the woman without having to tell the reader what it is. The exaggeration makes the case all by itself. But perhaps an additional analogy would make her character trait even clearer; is the woman slow and plodding, or is she vain and self-important? Perhaps her husband adds, **"This is dinner at the neighbors, not the Oscar's Red Carpet parade."** O.K., now my vote goes for vanity.

2. Physical characteristics related to the story.

Inexperienced writers tend to confine their characterization to obvious physical features, facial gestures, hair, size, bust, beard, prowess, etc. Instead of using such tedious descriptions, consider using traits that relate to the story. In a scene about seduction, for instance, you might give the man a deep baritone voice, or, if you want to make it really tough for him, a squeaky high-pitched voice. An adventure/survival story might feature a woman with a leg deformity. A legal thriller might benefit from a lawyer who stuttered, or a judge who was blind. A murder mystery may have a character that is psychologically disturbed, and it might be the detective rather than the suspect. A character's posture might be important, for example,

The body of a boxer a decade too long in the business, or
The backbone of a Master Sargent in the face of a new recruit.

You get the idea.

3. Contrast.

Contrast is the technique of assigning a character a trait that is inconsistent with other traits. Examples include:

- **A man in a three-piece pin striped suit with muddy shoes.**
- **An elegant woman at a formal dinner party cleans her teeth at the table.**
- **A preacher with a foul mouth.**
- **A trial lawyer who stutters.**

Traits that contrast with other traits of the same character are unique and make the characters unique, and, even better, a bit mysterious.

4. Markers.

A marker is a trait that is easily recognized by the reader and whose association with the character passes the trait on to the character himself. Markers can be either unique traits or unique figures of speech.

a. **Trait Markers.** There are hundreds of trait markers, for example: the choice of clothing; the appearance or location of an office or home; hobbies or activities; preferred food and restaurants; organizations or associations; favorite movies, TV shows, songs, books; a brand of beer or vintage of wine; one's social relationships; club memberships, and one's education. Basically, any trait that sets a character apart from other characters.

b. **Speech Markers.** Examples include one's choice of words, vocabulary, grammar, use of clichés, jargon, or vulgarity. Sarcasm and cynicism are also speech markers. A stutter or a lisp can be a marker. Verbosity or terseness can become a marker.

Markers are helpful in portraying characters as unique and distinguishing them from all other characters. In some cases, markers can also be useful in advancing the plot. For example, a lawyer who is quadriplegic both distinguishes and challenges the character, particularly if, for example, that lawyer is defending a personal injury lawsuit brought by another quadriplegic who is trying to prove he is disabled and unable to work in order to gain sympathy with a jury.

As helpful as markers are, their use also carries a modest risk. Readers want immediacy; they want to see the characters on stage in action, and they do not want tedious descriptions. An adequate description of a character's office, for example, may include only a mention of a desk, which, if small and metallic says one thing about the character, but if large and ornate says quite another. Avoid a description of the entire room; that's not necessary (at least not all at once) and readers do not have patience for it.

Character markers should hold true throughout the book, or they confuse the reader and lose their descriptive value. If a character is "marked" by poor grammar, that marker must stay with him. If his grammar periodically transcends to that of a college professor, the initial use of poor grammar becomes meaningless.

5. Ever-fascinating dialogue.

Dialogue is covered in Chapter 12, but I include a brief discussion here because of its importance in characterization, particularly as respects the character's emotions and state of mind. Consider the following statement,

"What a fool you are -- just like our father!"

This statement reveals two important character traits about the speaker: he hates his father and he doesn't get along with his brother. The reader learns all this from a single sentence uttered by the character himself. And consider how hard it would be to use narrative to portray the extent of the young man's hatred for both his father and his brother as well as it is portrayed in this single oral outburst. Dialogue is the one chance a writer has to get inside a character's head without the use of an omniscient narrator. In dialogue, everything a character says comes directly from his brain, so it is a very effective way to portray a character's inner feelings. Dialogue becomes the gate through which the writer invites the reader into the minds of his characters.

Chapter 2 Drill

Write a brief scene, using either narrative or dialogue that portrays a compelling character. The scene must contain conflict, emotion, and artistic vision.

CHAPTER 3

Emotion and Passion

Emotion is a prime driver of good characterization.

The human brain plays strange tricks on us, and we need to expose one of the most devious of these tricks before we can really understand human emotion. Our brains have actually led us to believe that we humans are able to make thoughtful decisions to guide our lives based on reason and logic. Wow, imagine that – if only it were true. Far from the truth, it is passion and emotion that rule the world. We love, envy, hate, and destroy each other not because doing so is logical or rational but because our passions and emotions inevitably control our thought processes. The primary role logic plays is to self-justify what our emotions have already instructed us to do.

Interesting philosophy, albeit a bit fatalistic, but why is it relevant in a book about how to write novels? The answer is that a writer who does not understand the role emotion plays in the lives of real people cannot possibly understand how to write about emotion in a literary work. We tend to think of emotion only as a condition that follows some event in our lives; that is, we become sad when a loved one dies or happy when a child graduates from college. And of course, that's quite true, but it is the lesser half of the whole story. Emotion is not just the result of some event, very often emotion is what causes the event in the first place. We envy an acquaintance's success at something we failed to accomplish on our own, so we snub our noses at him, or worse. Emotion can also be both the cause and effect of human actions. For example, anger precipitates a vicious attack which in turn results in a feeling of remorse. That is, anger causes an action, and remorse results from the action.

We writers must appreciate the multidimensional roles played by human emotions if our characters are going to become real, compelling people.

- On the one hand, our characters' emotions must play a dominant role in guiding their behavior. If they merely run through their literary roles making logical, rational decisions, they will be unreal, dull and boring,
- Likewise, our characters must demonstrably show their emotions following significant events that affect their lives. If their reactions to major events are unemotional, they will likewise be unreal, dull and boring.

Which takes us to another common shortcoming I see in the manuscripts of budding writers – the characters do not show enough emotion. Memorable people have passionate hopes and dreams; they have flaws, they are complex, and they are deeply human. Emotion is where the reader and the character become one, where the reader feels exactly what the character feels. Emotion is what makes the reader want to jump up on his chair to cheer on the disadvantaged, or angrily throw rotten eggs at the bully. Emotionally flat characters are like flat line EKGs – they're dead.

Writing intense emotion cannot happen if the writer is a dispassionate storyteller. Quite the contrary, the writer must deeply feel his own characters' emotions on a very personal level. If the writer does not cry when the characters cry, does not laugh when the characters laugh, does not tense up when the characters are threatened, then true emotion is missing. That's how I know that I have written a memorable scene – when I break into tears myself at the misery I have created for my protagonist.

Emotion is about contrasts, extremes, passionate arousals, all shown through real life vignettes, never merely described in words. The main characters are often at extremes, lovable or despicable, but with depth and supercharged emotions. They must be flawed, real people who could live next door. We writers must get inside their minds and bodies and bring the reader inside with us.

Dramatic emotional swings take the characters on a roller coaster ride until the very end of the story when all conflict is finally resolved, either by success or failure. Storytelling is about reversals. We love to see humble people get big, big people get knocked down, and the knocked get up to fight again. Characters struggle for success, and then they crash and burn, find redemption, crash and burn again, and maybe get back on top again.

Let me give you some examples I have written to illustrate my point. The first example includes two scenes where my self-assigned task is to paint an image of love and sadness. Both scenes depict identical facts. You decide which scene you like better and why. The second example includes two scenes about anger, also written twice for purposes of comparison.

Example 1A – Love and Sadness

As Sarah spread her husband's ashes at the base of a magnificent oak tree in the middle of a field filled with the yellow daffodils he had planted years before, a single tear rained down her cheek, signaling the sad end of her long and happy marriage.

Example 1B – Love and Sadness

From her small cottage, Sarah noticed the first of the yellow daffodils popping open in the field just beyond her garden. The luminous rays of the early morning sun saturated the delicate flowers and turned them into a field of gold. Anton had planted them himself, thousands of them, a birthday present for Sarah. The long, lonely winter was finally over.

Sarah carefully collected the ceramic urn from her mantel, cradled it tightly against her breasts and strolled outside, past her garden and into the great field beyond.

"Mother," shouted a male voice from the doorway to the cottage, "It's time."

"Time," she thought, "the young know so little about time," and, without responding, she continued walking through the field towards a magnificent oak, older, she imagined, than all living humanity. One last journey with the only man she had ever loved.

Example 2A -- Anger

Sam walked into the room and noticed the shit-eating grin on his brother's face. "Don't be a jerk," he said, as he sat down at the table and bit off a wad of tobacco.

Example 2B -- Anger

Sam jumped up from his chair and glared back at his brother's shit-eating grin, now only inches away. "You're a goddamn liar," he yelled at the top of his voice and spit a wad of tobacco directly into his eye.

So, which Sarah do you feel closer to? Which Sam is the more emotive? The facts in each scene are identical; the only difference is the level of emotion created by the manner of presenting the facts. There's nothing wrong about either of the first examples. They're both nicely written and grammatically correct. The problem is that the absence of real emotion leaves the reader in his chair calmly perusing words that are rather bland. The second examples do a better job of capturing the reader's attention and getting him out of his comfortable chair and into the story. This is where we want our readers to habituate.

The bottom line: emotion matters.

Chapter 3 Drill

Identify any human emotion and then write a brief scene, using either narrative or dialogue, that fully captures that emotion. The scene itself must depict the emotion, and you may not either identify the emotion specifically or use any word synonymous with the emotion in writing the scene. The goal is for any person reading the scene for the first time to immediately identify the emotion you have selected.

CHAPTER 4

Captivating Story

A captivating story is a principal component of all good fiction as well as a prime force in creating an enjoyable experience for the reader.

T his is the most readily understood of the Seven Principles because, as readers, we all have well-founded opinions about what makes for a captivating story. Yet, it is still worth a couple of pages to specify and briefly discuss the major ingredients of a captivating story so they are ready in mind as you plan your storyline. And notice that I used the word "storyline," not "plot," because, in this chapter, I ignore the role conflict plays. I do that to emphasize that, while it is impossible to have a captivating story without literary conflict, the converse is not true; just because literary conflict is present does not guarantee a captivating story. What else is required?

Here's my shopping list.

1. The story must be entertaining.

This is an absolute. Above all, readers want to be entertained and enjoy a brief vacation for their brains. Of course, everyone enjoys different forms of entertainment, and not every genre appeals to every reader. But whatever genre you choose must appeal to the entertainment interests of that type of reader. As we have seen, conflict helps, and emotion helps, but more is needed. The story itself must capture the imagination and fancies of the readers so they will be entertained.

2. The story must be imaginative.

None of us are interested in reading the mundane stories we have all heard many times before, maybe even experienced ourselves. We want stories that are unique and imaginative, stories that take us places we have never been, except maybe in our dreams. A good writer let's his imagination run wild. Wild but not crazy.

3. The story should be amazing.

We all like to read stories that are remarkable, incredible, astounding, even mind-blowing. Amazing, yes, impossible, no. A writer can take his reader to the edge of believability, but not past it. Readers will quickly lose interest if they do not believe the story is real, if it could not happen, perhaps to their next-door neighbor. Believability is equally applicable to science fiction; the reader must be able to believe the story could happen, even if he is not quite sure how.

4. The story must have suspense.

By suspense, I am not referring merely to stories that are frightening or apprehensive, like thrillers, although certainly those terms qualify. Rather I am intending a broader definition of the term, for example, exciting, enthralling, gripping, and dynamic. No matter which genre is selected, the reader should be kept on the edge of his seat by a story that does not let up. No wasted space or tiresome chatter. No long plateaus.

5. The story should be filled with mystery.

Here again I am not referring to the genre of mystery thrillers; to the contrary, mystery should be an integral part of all genres. The definition I use includes enigma, puzzle, conundrum, secret, unsolved, not understood. I discuss this in greater detail in Chapter 5.

6. The story should have periodic surprises.

Readers love to be surprised, and surprises are easy to create. Take any incident and consider how the incident should most likely be resolved. Then do exactly the opposite.

7. The story should be active but reflective.

A great literary novel is entertaining, but it is even better if it stimulates the reader to explore some aspect of the social order or the human condition. A story that is relevant to one or more of the issues of the day has an added chance of becoming captivating. Even if the story itself does not require addressing some current hot topic, it is easy to insert one. For example, a murder mystery may be very entertaining on its own, but it becomes even more interesting if the murder is related to some issue of the day, e.g., racial tension, gay lesbian issues, religious intolerance, white supremacy, school bullying, gun violence, and the like.

In the end, you don't really need much help from me to plan a captivating story. And you will know whether you have succeeded. All you really need to do is keep these concepts in mind as you develop your plot.

Chapter 4 Drill

Write a short plotline for a captivating story. The plotline should demonstrate that the story will be entertaining, imaginative, amazing, suspenseful, and reflective.

Mystery and Suspense

> Mystery and suspense are prime
> drivers of a captivating story.

Mystery and suspense are the lures that keep readers turning the pages because they are dying to find out what happens. Mystery enables the writer to stimulate the reader's curiosity, and suspense keeps him aroused throughout the book.

Mystery results when any event, object or character presents features that are obscure and arouse curiosity or speculation. Suspense results when an event is exciting, enthralling, gripping, or dynamic, when the reader is kept on the edge of his seat by a story that does not let up. No wasted space or tiresome chatter. No long plateaus. The writer creates a situation that requires resolution and then, instead of resolution, the problem is prolonged and exacerbated. Danger (either physical or mental) is always present. If one danger is averted, another quickly emerges. If the protagonist takes appropriate action to end the danger, his actions must not be enough, and the danger must persist. In our real world we all do everything possible to avoid danger; in our books we never want it to end.

I often use the words "mystery" and "suspense" synonymously

although in reality "mystery" refers to the unknown whereas "suspense" refers to the emotional state of anxiety that a mystery produces. In any event, to avoid tediously using both words together all the time, let's treat the words as synonymous for this chapter and focus on the important roles they play in all good literary works.

Mystery as a literary tool is used in two distinct ways. First, the story itself should be mysterious in the sense that the author reveals information to the reader slowly and incompletely to keep the reader speculating about the ultimate outcome – good, bad or in between. Will our protagonist rise up from the depth of despair and realize his dreams, or will he crash and burn in ignominy?

Second, tidbits of mystery should be inserted as "teasers" throughout the book to keep the reader turning pages long after he had promised to clean the garage. I tell my students to think of the last paragraph in any given chapter as really the first paragraph in the next chapter. In the nonfiction world, proper grammatical structure requires that every chapter have a beginning, a middle, and an end, in essence a self-contained section of a complete book. If this were how fiction were written, a chapter would begin with a character wanting something, following which he acts to overcome obstacles to achieve his want, following which he either succeeds or fails. The chapter ends, and the writer moves on to the next chapter.

This approach does not work in fiction. If every chapter has a natural end to it, what reason does the reader have to keep going? A natural end to a chapter is a natural end for the reader as well. But that's not what we writers want; we're all too happy to lure our readers to ignore their messy garages in favor of an extended sojourn fully immersed in our eloquent words.

To make this happen most chapters should finish with a beginning rather than an end. While the conflict that dominates any given chapter may get resolved, or partially resolved, the next conflict should generally be introduced at the end of the current chapter rather than at the beginning of the next chapter. The next conflict can either be directly stated or at least hinted before the chapter ends. I generally prefer hinting because a hint produces more mystery. Either way, the chapter ends with a lure that hooks our hapless reader so he forgets all about his garage.

Another tactic is to create multiple mysteries all occurring at the same time and then prolong resolution even further by skipping around from one mystery to another throughout the novel. A mystery that is left unresolved at the end of Chapter 1, for instance, is set aside in Chapter 2, which, instead of moving the first mystery towards resolution, introduces a second mystery, which likewise is not resolved in Chapter 2. Now there are two reasons for the reader to keep going, not just one. Chapter 3 may return to the first problem but will again leave it unresolved before Chapter 4 takes over. The order in which chapters are organized in fiction is almost never chronological. Instead, chapters should be ordered, in part, to achieve maximum mystery for the reader. A little diabolical, I admit, but it works.

I used the word "danger" above to describe the nature of the suspense. In doing so I use an expansive definition of "danger" to include both the fear of physical danger and also a conscious concern about a challenge that may be entirely mental.

Examples of Mental Danger:

1. **Will Brent make the Olympic hockey team despite all the physical hardships he has been forced to endure?**
2. **Will Sarah overcome her lifelong learning disability and receive a scholarship to Princeton?**
3. **Can Zack find happiness despite years of drug addiction and incarceration?**

The "dangers" Brent, Sarah and Zack face is loss of their fervently held dreams despite years of struggles to make them come true. These are not physical dangers, but the mental despair they may endure through failure is every bit as devastating as physical injury. Be they physical or mental, these "dangers" create mystery and suspense for the reader.

Let's look at a few examples of mystery.

Example 1:

Megan pried open the dusty old trunk at the back of the attic. The hinges squeaked like the wheels of a freight train, and she paused for a moment to listen for any stirring from her mother's bedroom directly below. She hadn't heard, the deaf old hag.

Three sentences, three mysteries. What was in the trunk? Why was it so secret? Why did Megan despise her mother? Good questions, but good writers will not give good answers. The writer may show the reader what was in the trunk, but its significance will remain a mystery. The reader will see only a few vague clues about why it was such a secret, and the reader will almost surely not fully understand why Megan so despised her mother until the very last chapter.

Example 2:

The street was empty and dark. Entirely normal, I told myself, as I inched my way towards the side door of the old abandoned bookstore.

One sentence, three mysteries. What was he doing all alone, in town, late at night? Was everything really as normal as he tried to convince himself? What secrets might be uncovered in the abandoned bookstore?

Example 3:

As the first of the cold December winds battered the ancient timbers of the old prairie church I had served for nearly two decades, little did I know that the furious winter that was

about to begin would see three men and a child die in this peaceful, sacred place.

Would this be a good first paragraph for a murder mystery?

Example 4:

As Josh ambled through the kitchen to grab another beer from the fridge, he noticed a small manila envelope partially tucked under the keyboard of his father's computer. Easily visible was the return address, The Federal Bureau of Investigation.

Would this be a good last paragraph in a chapter? Would the reader want to know why the letter was hidden under the keyboard? Would the reader be dying to know what was in the letter from the FBI? Creating mystery is important; keeping mystery alive is essential. The good writer postpones unveiling the real story as long as possible. Maybe, for example, in the next chapter when Josh passes through the kitchen a few hours later, the letter is gone. But no one had been home, so who took it? Does he dare ask his father about the letter? If he does, what are his father's non-verbal responses to the question? Does Josh ask his mother about the letter? Does Josh check his father's text messages and find a strange communication? The mystery keeps getting bigger, and the clues keep getting more intriguing and oblique.

One final word on mystery -- it should go to the heart of the story. Mysteries that are unrelated to the story (unless they are intentional decoys) serve no purpose. For instance, in Example 1 above, if the secret contents of the trunk do not take the reader to the heart of the plot, the scene has no value. On the other hand, if the story delves into a long-estranged relationship between mother and daughter and the trunk hides secrets that may shed some light on that relationship, then it serves nicely to hook the reader into what may be a powerful story about two compelling women, albeit women with serious character flaws.

Chapter 5 Drill

Write the first and last sentences of the first chapter of a novel of any genre of your choosing. The goal is to use mystery and suspense to hook the reader into the story after only one sentence and to keep the reader aroused so he will immediately want to read the second chapter.

CHAPTER 6

Artistic Vision

> Artistic vision is the lens through which the reader becomes emotionally attached to, or repulsed by, the main characters.

T hink of seeing the world with Superman eyes, or, as I like to suggest, with Writers' Eyes that see things no one else notices. Think of turning black and white into a rainbow of color. And, as we discussed in Chapter 2, think of yourself as an artist who paints pictures in words, an artist who sees deep into the heart and soul of his subject and uses words to paint vibrant, color-saturated, and profoundly penetrating images for all to see.

Let's return to our discussion of the Mona Lisa because a solid understanding of the qualities that make this painting both mesmerizing and absurdly valuable is essential to your ability to paint exquisite word images of your own characters. In the end, the qualities of great art are almost identical to the qualities of great literature.

What do you see in this painting? What is this woman's story? What are the qualities that make it a great painting? Does the painting draw you into Mona Lisa's world? Does it stimulate your reflectivity?

A good exercise I ask my students to undertake is to write a paragraph in which they use words to paint the image of Mona Lisa that they see in the painting. The idea is to capture the inner spirit of the woman without actually identifying the spirit they are describing. Nor do the students' interpretations of the woman have to agree with those da Vinci thought he was painting. da Vinci has no more right as a painter than you do as a writer to tell his audience what they are supposed to see. Artists and writers paint images as they see them, but their audience gets to interpret those images as it chooses. Thus, the goal I give my students is to use words to paint an image through which all other students in the class can readily identify the character trait being depicted. The image can be painted using either narrative or dialogue. Here are some examples.

Example 1:

Mona Lisa was an ordinary woman dressed simply in black and sitting stiffly on a bench with an unpretentious smile and shallow, focused eyes.

I hope you quickly recognize this as a poor attempt. As I explain in the next chapter, this is "telling," not "showing." In addition, the sentence merely describes her exterior appearance and does not take the reader inside Mona Lisa's soul; it does not explain why she has so captured the hearts of the millions of people who have studied her portrait.

Example 2:

She glowed warm with a candlelit serenity that betrayed her deep haunting eyes. And her smile, oh that endearing, powerful smile; God help the poor soul who is want to cause her pain.

This description is improved because at least the second sentence begins to get into the heart of the woman and take the reader along. It is still more superficial than I like to see.

Example 3:

Her smile radiated the power of a queen and the cunning of a mystic. God help the poor soul who is want to cause her pain.
Example 3 does the best job at depicting the woman's inner self, at least how I choose to interpret it. Notice how elimination of all the adjectives and adverbs actually strengthens the image. The descriptive phrases in Example 2, "Glowed warm," "candlelit serenity," "haunting eyes," and "endearing powerful smile" are nicely written, but they do not get under Mona Lisa's skin and into her heart, and they say very little about who this woman really is. In Chapter 10, I devote several pages to a discussion of the disadvantages of using adjectives as a primary vehicle to describe a character. This series of examples is further illustrative of that point.

Example 4:

"I don't buy a word of her story," Sarge said. "She's got liars' eyes, looks right through you when she talks."
"Yeah," Jordi replied, "And that holier-than-thou grin on her face; what a bitch. She's hiding something."
"Yeah, like what the hell she did with the murder weapon."
This is obviously an extremely fanciful interpretation of the Mona Lisa, one that no scholar would ever condone. I include it here only because 1) it illustrates how dialogue can be used to paint an image of a character, and 2) it satisfies my love for wild imagination, a trait that serves fiction writers quite nicely.

Let's do one more exercise to advance my thesis that artistic vision is a valuable skill for writers. The drill is the same -- to write a short description of the photograph below, one that captures the spirit of the building, not its exterior appearance. Again, artistic vision is the call of the day.

Example 1

We drove across the South Dakota prairie and, in the middle of an empty field, observed a white clapboard church with a short, squat steeple topped with a thin white cross.

Example 1 is again an obviously poor attempt because it does little more than describe the exterior walls of this church. The reader could care less.

Example 2

That little church on the prairie was like a stubborn old spinster, lonely and frail, yet still ministering kindness to the few congregants who paid her an occasional visit.

This is better. We now begin to see the inside of a charming building that serves an important need to its rural congregants. But it is still not strong enough because it relies solely on a narrative description to portray the spirit of the building.

Example 3

For almost a half century the Reverend Nathaniel Mitchell ministered kindness and compassion from that old clapboard church on the prairie, and in return, for one hour every week, virtually every farm family in the county filled the lovely old structure with song and celebration of the Word of the Lord.

Example 3 is better yet because the church is described not by narrative description but by activities that have taken place inside the church for many years. Note again that, even with all of the adjectives and similes removed, the personality of the church is nicely portrayed.

The point of this drill is to demonstrate that the reader is more interested in what goes on inside a building than what the building looks like. What happens inside describes the building far better than how it appears externally. Example 2 is a good description, and it gives at least a slight hint about what goes on inside, but Example 3 is by far the best at capturing the real essence of this church.

And, because I do not want writers to leave their imaginations in their desk drawers, here's another, more fanciful, description of the church.

Example 4:

As nighttime suffocated the last feeble rays of a December sun and the first of the cold winter winds battered the ancient timbers of the old prairie church I had served for nearly two decades, little did I know that the furious winter that was about to begin would see three men and a child die in this peaceful, sacred place.

What a great first sentence for a murder mystery! More on that in Chapter 12.

THE OTHER FIVE SENSES

So far in this chapter I have focused exclusively on vision. I know, that's all the title of this chapter promises. But I want to take you on a brief side trip, a quick tour of our other five other senses: touch, taste, smell, sound, and ESP.

In order to give our readers the most enjoyable experience possible, we writers must appeal to all of our readers' senses, just as we all do in real life. We must paint images not merely of what we see, but also of what we feel, smell, hear, and foretell. Consider how important it may be to describe:

- **how a woman smells,**
- **how the face of a baby feels,**
- **how a powerful thunderstorm sounds,**
- **the sense of imminent danger on a dark street corner,**
- **the sounds a baby makes playing with his rattle in a crib,**
- **the odors of death,**
- **the odors of a basement cellar,**
- **the feel of a handshake**
- **the taste of a food item,**
- **the sense of something in the air: a foreboding, an excitement, a brewing storm.**

Chapter 6 Drill

Select either of the pictures contained in this chapter and write no more than one page, using either narrative or dialogue, to capture your interpretation of the picture. Let your vision and imagination roam wild.

Showing Versus Telling

> Showing, not telling, is the primary tool
> that brings the reader into the heat of
> the action to experience the story first
> hand as it unfolds.

"Telling" is supplying information to the reader directly from the narrator or, worse, from the author himself. This is one of the most common mistakes made by inexperienced writers. The reader wants to experience the scene first hand with his own eyes; he absolutely does not want to be told about it by anyone else. He particularly does not want to be told about it by the author. Telling him about the scene destroys the reader's experience.

Let me offer you a choice.

Your daughter is competing for the state figure skating championship. You, the mother, can either stay home to prepare dinner for the family and listen to a detailed description of the event from your husband, or you can forget about the dinner and go to the ice arena and watch it yourself.

Hard choice?

As easy as that choice is, the hard truth is that we writers do not give our readers the ability to make the choice. We make the decision whether to force them to listen to the husband's summary or take them to the ice arena where they experience the competition personally. Why, you ask, would any writer decide to tell the reader about the skating championship instead of allowing the reader to see it with his own eyes?

I'll answer my own question in two words: laziness or forgetfulness.

First, laziness. It's far easier to tell than to show, particularly because showing includes both showing the scene and also showing the emotions of the scene. Consider the following examples.

Example 1

She skated beautifully, poetry in motion, strong and sure, determined to win the championship."

Example 2

There she stood, alone, in the middle of an ice rink the size of Montana. Silence reigned as thousands of spectators shifted in their seats and waited anxiously for the music to begin. For the last skater to perform. Her face spoke of fear, and her thighs tensed as she rose onto the tips of her skates and gracefully lifted her arms over her head like the halo of an angel. A moment later the blare of the trumpet from Tchaikovsky's 4th filled the arena, and the fear in her eyes evaporated and seamlessly morphed into the grit of unrelenting determination. She skated effortlessly, like a soaring eagle, as five thousand mesmerized heads rotated in synchronized motion as she circled the arena. A double toe loop was all that remained in her routine. Her legs pumped hard as she built up speed leading into the jump. A split second lasted an hour as she rotated high in the air, once around, twice around, and landed like a butterfly on a rose petal. Perfection. Until it wasn't. The toe of her right skate grabbed the ice and threatened to hurl her towards what, for

a lesser talent, would certainly have been a death spiral. Not this night. Not this girl. She reflexively shifted her weight onto her left leg, allowing the right skate to release its death grip and, with barely a detectable wiggle, she glided to mid ice for a final, perfect pirouette. The audience, en masse, leapt to their feet and their spontaneous applause shook the arena to its foundation. And her face spoke of elation.

How much harder it is to write version 2. Trust me, it's worth the effort.

Second, forgetfulness. There is another explanation for the "telling" problem besides laziness, and it's easily understood. We writers almost invariably start with a story, often one that has long been on our minds, so it is entirely natural that we think of ourselves as storytellers.

But telling stories is not our job. The real job of writers, like that of an artist, is to paint images that draw the reader into our characters, like da Vinci draws us into the Mona Lisa. Has any reader of this book seen a single word written by da Vinci to describe his Mona Lisa? da Vinci tells us nothing about her. He does not have to; da Vinci shows us the Mona Lisa so we can see her with our own eyes, experience her emotions, and be drawn into her world. To be sure, a great storyteller can add color to his narrative and make it interesting, but he can never, I mean never, make it as interesting as seeing the story unfold with one's own eyes.

Here's the solution. Somewhere in the early stages of planning our novels, we writers must move beyond the storyline that we have long been contemplating. The time for that is during the preparation of the chapter outline. As I explain in Chapter 9, I encourage all writers, even seasoned published writers, to prepare chapter outlines. I present my case for that later; for now, just accept my thesis that the preparation of a chapter outline gives the writer an opportunity to plan how he is going to "show" the scene or scenes that will occur in each chapter. This is an excellent opportunity to transform ourselves from storytellers to story-showers. From authors to artistic directors. This is an opportune time to decide how to make our stories come alive, to take them away from the campfire and put them instead on center stage.

There are several areas where writers seem to be particularly prone to forget about showing versus telling.

1. Describing our characters' feelings.

We are often tempted to tell the reader exactly how a character feels, that is, to identify the emotion we want the character to have at that moment. This is ineffective. Consider the following two examples:

Example 1A

"Zack was really angry at his brother for lying to him."

Example 1B

Zack leapt out of his chair and glared straight into his brother's shit-eating grin, now only inches away. "You're a goddamn liar," he yelled at the top of his voice and spit a wad of tobacco into his eye.

Example 2A

"Sarah was enormously saddened by the death of her husband."

Example 2B

"Almost nothing remained of his emaciated body. His 85 years had done what years do best, bring humility to the

greatest of warriors and to the meekest of men, all in equal doses. His wife nudged her body delicately onto his bed and wrapped her arms around his cold and clammy shoulders. 'What a gift,' she whispered into his lifeless ear, 'no woman has ever been happier. I would not trade away a minute of our life together, not even this one.'"

Which version of Zack is more convincing of the extent of Zack's anger? Which is more convincing of the enormity of Sarah's sadness? Which one draws the reader into the action? In versions 1A and 2A the author simply tells the reader what the characters' emotions are; in versions 1B and 2B the reader sees the emotions with his own eyes.

2. Providing descriptions of characters.

Narrative descriptions are fine as far as they go, but they do not go very far. It has been well documented that almost all of us learn better when we see something than when we hear it. As a trial lawyer I knew that any given juror would actually remember only about 10% of what I said in court. Thus I repeated important points many times during a trial. Lawyers can get away with repetition in court, but writers cannot.

The other tactic I used in court was to prepare visual exhibits that I could offer into evidence and "show" the jury during trial and during my final argument. Visual exhibits have a much better chance of being remembered by most jurors. Jurors who hear lawyers "tell" them something, remember it less well that jurors who see what lawyers have "shown" them. Our readers react just as jurors do – they invariably remember something we show them far better than something we tell them. To borrow from the examples of Zack and Sarah above, which version of Zack's anger is more likely to remain with the reader? Which version of Sarah's sadness is likely to be more memorable?

Here are several additional comparisons.

Example 3A

Gene was the perfect father, totally dedicated to his son.

Example 3B

Gene always left home by 5 a.m. so he could finish his work and be home by 4 o'clock to coach his son's little league team.

In Example 3A there is nothing for the reader to see, nothing to feel. The reader is simply told about Gene's qualities as a father. It's unconvincing. Just a few additional words make all the difference in Example 3B, where the reader is invited into Gene's life to see something Gene does to qualify him as a terrific father. The reader experiences what he can see; he does not experience what he is told.

Example 4A

Mary was extremely nervous about her job interview.

Example 4B

Pacing back and forth across her bedroom, Mary stared obsessively at the text icon on her iPhone. "Damn. They promised to call by 4 o'clock."

Example 4A is telling; 4B is showing.

2. Providing descriptions of an object or setting.

As with characters, writers are often tempted to provide a detailed narrative description of an object or setting, rather than create a scene that shows the object or setting. Consider the following example.

Example 5A

He sat remorsefully behind his large, ornate desk, which was entirely bare but for the gold-framed picture of his wife on their wedding day.

Example 5B

Seated at his desk, where it had all happened, where he had tried so hard to make things right, he eyed the picture of his wife, his favorite picture of her on the happiest day of his life. Maybe, he thought, his only happy day. He pulled open a drawer to retrieve a small yellow pad and pen but instead was confronted by the soothing snigger of his father's old Beretta.

Example 5A focuses on telling the reader about the desk and the picture of the man's wife, neither of which interests the reader in the least. The one important word in the sentence, "remorsefully," is practically hidden from view, and most likely will be glossed over and lost. The reader does not really care about the objects; the reader cares about the man. The desk and the photo are only important insofar as they help define the man's emotional state, in this example, in the throes of a contemplated suicide.

Example 6A

The thunderheads exploded like bombs in a war zone.

Example 6B

I was caught, alone, on the prairie I'd known all my life, but which now turned threatening and alien. As I pumped

the pedals on my bike with every ounce of energy I had left, lightning bolts bombarded me with long exploding tentacles. My calves stung from voodoo needles I was certain forecasted my imminent death. Another half mile. I just had to make it.

Example 6A is nicely written and adequately describes a very stormy night. I don't really object to it, even though it is an example of a narrated description; the simile saves the sentence from an "F" for "telling." But maybe the writer wants something more to bring the scene to life, and, more importantly, to bring the reader into the scene. Example 6B accomplishes this because the reader is drawn into scene by his empathy for the frightened young boy as he frantically pedals his bike toward the safety of home.

The point of these comparisons is to illustrate how much more powerfully a writer can describe a scene by inserting action into the scene. Or conversely, and more importantly, how a scene can be useful in describing the state of mind of a character.

Chapter 7 Drill

Write a short sentence that "tells" any fact you wish. (Examples: I saw a powerful tornado quickly approaching my farmhouse; Sarah was a beautiful woman, perfect complexion, gorgeous blond hair and a perfect hourglass figure; Zack was an evil man through and through.) Pick any subject you wish. Then write no more than one paragraph that "shows" what you "told."

CHAPTER 8

Anatomy of a Great Novel

To fully understand the Seven Principles of Literary Excellence it is helpful to appreciate their synergetic relationship with one another. By analogy, a physician who understands the role of each of the body's vital organs individually but not how they work together cannot provide ideal care for his patients. Similarly, a writer who understands the Seven Principles individually but not how they fit together will be disadvantaged in writing great fiction. The Seven Principles work together as a team to produce quality fiction.

Physicians learn how human organs work together in part by studying anatomy. Let's follow their lead and spend a few pages considering the anatomy of good fiction. I'm treading a bit on uncharted territory here because I'm unaware of any creative writing instructor or author who has attempted to describe an anatomical chart of good fiction. I make that attempt here. First a word of caution. While readers may be tempted to find perceived fallacies in the chart, let me encourage all to accept it for what it is — a vehicle to illustrate how the Seven Principles fit together synergistically in a novel. For that purpose, at least, it matters not whether there is universal acceptance of the accuracy of my anatomical chart.

My thesis is that there are two primary components in all good novels, compelling characters and a captivating story. Accepting this thesis necessarily means that all seven principles must promote one or both of these components. My Anatomical Chart of a Great Novel shows exactly how this occurs.

Spend a few minutes studying the chart on the next page. There are several interesting take-aways from this chart.

1. The chart is helpful in visualizing how the Seven Principles interact with each other to build a good novel. This lends perspective to the writer as he creates scenes, knowing how each of the principles we have discussed (and tools we are about to discuss) impact the novel as a whole.

2. Most of the seven principles promote characterization whereas only two, conflict and mystery, promote the quality of the story. That's because compelling characters are more important to readers than a captivating story. A bland story with interesting characters stands a better chance of success than bland characters with an interesting story. The message is clear – as writers we should focus more on our characters and less on our stories.

3. The showing versus telling problem affects characterization more than the quality of the story. Mystery and suspense, for example, are not at risk for telling because, with mystery, the writer is careful to avoid both telling and showing. The other elements of a captivating story are conceptual rather than stylistic. In other words, many of the characteristics that make a story captivating are determined before the first word is written, as the writer lays out the plot and plans a storyline. That is to say, a story becomes entertaining, imaginative, amazing, and reflective mostly by virtue of the qualities of the story itself and less by the manner in which the story is told.

Anatomical Chart of a Great Novel

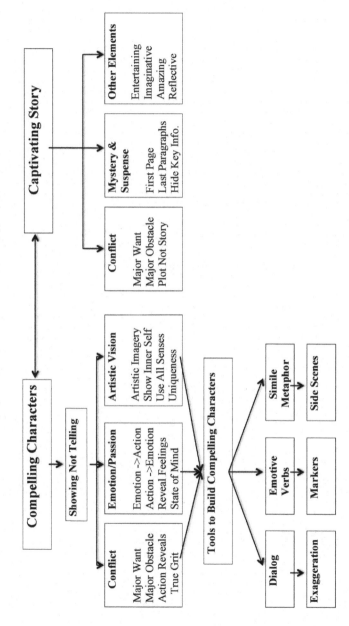

Part Two

Successful Writing
Techniques

CHAPTER 9

How to Get Started; Organization and Planning

Writing a novel or short story is a major undertaking, and the author must be well disciplined and prepare a clear plan of action. This starts with carving out enough time to complete the project. Make writing a high priority. Scheduled it on the calendar with everything else important in one's life. Pick regular days each week for writing and stick to them. If it isn't a priority, your project will languish and you will perennially feel guilty and frustrated.

Planning one's writing schedule is important but planning out the project itself is even more important. Take time at the outset, before writing a single sentence, to organize one's thoughts and develop a plan of attack. Writing a complete novel is a challenging and complex organizational endeavor. Opportunities for missteps are numerous. I'm aware of some seasoned writers who do not engage in careful planning and feel comfortable clinking their keyboards as soon as they have a storyline in mind. Go ahead and try this if you want ... on your second novel. This approach may work for a few seasoned writers, but it is a formula for failure for almost everyone else.

What follows is my checklist of four pre-writing steps that I recommend for every writer. Following each one I provide examples of what is required, all of them based on my own novel, *The Litigators*. None of these pre-writing steps takes an inordinate amount of time to complete, and I have no doubt that the minimal investment of time dedicated to advanced planning will save copious time later on. And it will produce a far better novel.

1. The Storyboard

This is where the idea for the story is developed. While quite a bit of thought should be devoted to the storyline, a page or two is all that is needed. Here's a good outline for developing the storyline.

a. A good first step is to outline an idea that you believe will result in a captivating story, that is, one that is entertaining, imaginative, amazing, interesting, and compelling. Refer to Chapter 4 for a refresher on what exactly makes a story captivating.

b. Second, summarize the basic plot by identifying the main characters and both their dreams and the major obstacles that will threaten to destroy those dreams.

c. Third, the storyline must convince your most critical inner self that the main characters will be compelling and the story will be entertaining. Ideally, in literary fiction, the story will also address some aspect of the human condition or some current societal issue. The storyboard is where the author demonstrates how he will present and address those ideas.

d. Fourth, this is the ideal time to consider the book's marketability. If you have aspirations of submitting the book to traditional publishing houses, the book's market appeal will be of prime importance. For you it's all about the quality of your writing; for editors and literary agents it's all about sales. A great book with a small potential audience will generate little interest with traditional publishers. This is not to say that you should write for an audience; you should write for yourself. If the book you want to write has a small potential market, write it anyway.

e. The storyboard need not be longer than a single page, but it can be longer if the author believes more detail will help organize his thoughts.

Example of a Storyboard – *The Litigators*

Basic Plot:

This is an archetypical legal battle between good and evil, but with a twist – both parties to the lawsuit are good and both deserve to win. The evil that must be defeated is the myopic lawyers who view the lawsuit as a personal contest, a competition to be won or lost no matter how large the cost, no matter how severe the emotional toll on them or their clients. Ruthie Bergstrom, a beautiful young mother, develops a mysterious neurological illness. Is it a coincidence that she lives near an abandoned gas station where an experimental biological product has been used for environmental cleanup? The product was developed by Boyd Campbell, a brilliant professor of molecular biology at the University of Minnesota, and deeply committed to improving the environment. Dillon Love, a spirited young lawyer, takes on the largest law firm in Minnesota on her behalf. How far will he go for his client? How far will the defense go to bend the rules of ethics and stop him? How will Ruthie Bergstrom make ends meet if she loses the case? What if the lawsuit destroys the career of the brilliant university professor who has dedicated his life to improving the environment? What if the lawsuit bankrupts a good company that is dedicated to improving the environment? Can justice be won for either party without inflicting grave injustice on the other?

Main Characters:

- Ruthie Bergstrom, delightful mother and wife who becomes severely ill.
- Boyd Campbell, brilliant university professor dedicated to developing new scientific processes to clean up toxic waste sites, one of which is alleged to have caused the severe illness.
- Their male lawyers, Dillon Love and Henry Holton, who view litigation as a competition to be won at all costs.
- The only female lawyer, Allison Forbes, who tries unsuccessfully to steer her male counterparts to alter their scorched earth game plan and see the case from their clients' perspectives.

Wants and Obstacles:

The parties desperately want to know the truth surrounding Ruthie's illness and then quickly make peace with each other and move on with their lives. The obstacle they must overcome is their own lawyers' dominating arrogance and myopic desire to win their cases.

Resolution:

In the end, the lawsuit almost ruins the lives of both parties and their lawyers and depicts an American justice system that is flawed and must be improved.

2. Scene Charts

The next step I recommend is preparation of a chart of scenes. This is where the basic guts of the story are put together, but it is also where the writer, for the first time, is forced to address the Seven Principles of Literary Excellence and determine how they will all be incorporated into the book. I like to see scene charts prepared before chapter outlines because a scene chart is a short, easily used document that outlines the major scenes in chronological order. I like putting the scene chart together chronologically because that's the easiest way for the writer to envision the complete story. I think of a scene chart as a list of all the major conflicts that will drive the plot.

Besides serving as a basic outline of major conflicts, the scene chart also serves two other important functions. First, because it is short and easily viewed as a single document, it is useful in helping the writer determine the best order for the chapters, that is, the sequence in which the story will actually be told. The scene chart is prepared chronologically because that is the easiest way to do it, but only rarely does the actual novel proceed in chronological order. With the basic scenes laid out in a short table, deciding the order of chapters is easily accomplished.

The final purpose of a scene chart is to aid in determining point of view, who will tell the story and how the narrator will gain personal knowledge of the events. Often this decision is easy, but that's not always the case, particularly where stories take place over a long period of time or in different locales. In these cases, a single narrator may not have personal knowledge of all events and may be unable credibly to tell all that must be told. A scene chart is a convenient place for the writer to address this issue and make a decision about who and how the story will be narrated.

It's not important to identify every scene or chapter at this point. This is a working document that will grow over time as new ideas flow through your mind. While it's not important to have a complete list of all scenes, it is important to be specific in describing each scene that is identified. I have included the skeleton model for a sample scene chart below, again from my novel *The Litigators*. I recommend that you use the Tables program in Word or Pages as they are flexible and allow easy changes, deletions, and additions.

Example of a Scene Chart – *The Litigators* (first three chapters)

Scenes, listed in Chron. order	Date of Events in Scene	Chap. Num.	Locale of Scenes	Purpose of Chapter	Character Wants	Character Obstacles
Ruthie and George Bergstrom have an idyllic marriage and family. First signs of Ruthie's serious illness.	Jan. 15, 2000.	1	The Bergstrom home, local hospital.	Create emotional attachment between reader and Ruthie.	Live a happy, healthy family life.	Ruthie develops severe neurological illness.
Boyd Campbell is a dedicated husband and university professor trying to build a new company to clean up toxic waste sites.	Jan. 15, 2000	2	The Campbell home and neighborhood	Create emotional attachment between reader and Boyd Campbell.	Build a major business devoted to cleaning up toxic waste sites.	The possibility that Ruthie's illness was caused by his product.
Boyd Campbell meets with his lawyers to discuss public offering.	Jan. 15, 2000	3	Henry Holton's private club, Holton's office.	Portray Campbell's lawyer as arrogant.	Campbell wants public stock offering to raise money to build his company.	A potential legal claim against the company may foil the public offering.

When I create a chart like this, I start by listing all scenes in natural chronological order, even if that is not the order I intend to present them in the book. I like to include a date, or inclusive dates, when the action occurs because this is a helpful reference and insures a realistic timeline of events. I use the third column for reorganizing chapters out of chronological order. Note that in this example the first three chapters are placed in their natural chronological order. That happens to be the way I wanted it to work in my novel, but often the story is best told out of chronological sequence, and this chart offers a nice format for reordering the chapters when doing so makes the story more entertaining or suspenseful. In that case the chapter numbers would not be sequential in the chart as they are here. The fourth column merely lists the location of the scenes that make up the chapter.

The last three columns give direction to the writing. The fifth column forces the writer to specify the purpose of the chapter and thereby gives focus to his writing and aids in eliminating needless dialogue and narrative. The sixth and seventh columns are useful in building the storyline around major conflicts, which in my example involves conflict between the parties and their lawyers. Forcing writers to be specific about the nature of the wants and obstacles helps avoid the most common mistake inexperienced writers make, failing to include adequate conflict. Eliminating this misstep assists the writer both in building an emotional bond between the protagonist and the reader and also in fomenting the reader's antipathy towards the antagonist.

3. Character Profiles

Character profiles are brief paragraphs detailing:

- The unique traits that make all major characters interesting and compelling
- Their strengths and weaknesses

- Their likes and dislikes
- Their education
- Their social and cultural heritage: how they speak and think; how they dress; how they interact with others.
- I like to visualize what the character looks like, and generally I model it after someone, or some amalgam of people, I know so that I have a ready reference whenever I am writing a scene about the character, and particularly when I am writing dialogue.

Character profiles help in creating unique, distinct, and interesting characters. First-time authors tend to create characters that are nothing more than author-clones in different bodies. They talk and act much like the author himself, and worse, they all talk and act the same.

Character profiles also help in writing dialogue by insuring that all characters speak consistent with their background, education, perspectives, and ambitions.

Example of Character Profiles – *The Litigators*

Ruthie Bergstrom

> **The Plaintiff. High school education. Delightful mother of two young children and devoted wife of Arnie. Norwegian stoical attitude towards life. Extremely warm, kind and loveable person. Naïve and gullible.**

Boyd Campbell

> **The Defendant. Brilliant professor of molecular biology. Honest and honorable in all respects. PhD from Princeton University. Devoted husband to physician wife. Life devoted to protecting the environment. Great scientist but inexperienced businessman. Lured**

somewhat reluctantly by his commitment to the environment to leave the security of his laboratory at the University of Minnesota to form a company, EnviroClean, to commercialize a biological product he developed in his lab.

Dillon Love

Ruthie's lawyer. Young, struggling, but highly energetic lawyer who is drawn by his own unrealistic dreams of grandeur into pursuing a lawsuit on Ruthie's behalf against EnviroClean. He quickly finds himself immersed in legal quicksand, which ultimately destroys his law practice and his marriage.

Henry Holton

EnviroClean's lawyer. Brilliant trial lawyer with many years of success in courtrooms across the country. Arrogant to the max, he believes he is capable of winning any case he takes. His enormous ego blinds him to the real needs of his client and, in the process of representing EnviroClean's best interests, ends up bankrupting the company.

Allison Forbes

Holton's protégé and second chair for EnviroClean's defense. She is the only female lawyer and the only lawyer that really senses the injustice of the actions by Love and Holton, but, in the end is lured by her own career objections to champion Boyd's cause to the bitter end.

4. Chapter Outline

The final pre-writing step is the preparation of a chapter outline. Let's start by discussing the meaning of the word "chapter." Unfortunately, the word has no specific meaning, only a very generic one: "section of book," "part," "subdivision," etc. This definition is of no help whatsoever in deciding what or how much to include in any given chapter. And the many successful authors we have all read are no help either. Some chapters are single scenes, perhaps 5 to 10 pages in length; others are multiple scenes, occasionally more than 50 pages in length. Because there are no rules, writers can do whatever they want in deciding what to include in any given chapter.

I do have a recommendation. most readers prefer reasonably short chapters. They want the reading experience to be enjoying and relaxing, and that experience may be threatened if they are required to grind through a 50-page chapter before finding a convenient spot for a break. That converts the reading experience into a chore rather than an escape from all the other chores that fill their lives. And, since we are writing for readers, we should give readers what they want. In my opinion, ten to fifteen pages is a good target, although inevitably some chapters will necessarily be longer.

As for the content of any given chapter, again there are no rules, but again I have a recommendation. If a single scene will take ten pages to write, that is also a good place to end the chapter. If it takes several scenes to write ten to fifteen pages, then include them all in a single chapter. However, only those scenes that are related topically or temporally to each other should ordinarily be included in a single chapter. I know authors that do not follow this rule, but I think it's a good one, at least for previously unpublished writers.

Now let's talk about the chapter outline itself. One or two paragraphs describing the scenes in each chapter is sufficient. Each chapter summary should be consistent with the mission of the chapter as identified in the scene chart and should more fully develop the nature of the conflict that will dominate each chapter. In preparing each chapter summary, it is a good idea to consider all of the principles of literary excellence, particularly conflict, emotion, mystery and suspense. There are a number of reasons for preparing chapter outlines.

1. The outline allows the author to see the whole story and understand how all of the scenes fit together.
2. The outline gives focus to the writer and aids in avoiding tedious narrative and dialogue.
3. The outline serves as a checklist to insure compliance with the Seven Principles of Literary Excellence.
4. The outline makes the editing process easier by ensuring that changes made in one chapter are easily followed up with appropriate changes to other chapters.
5. Some literary agents and publishers want to see chapter outlines.
6. Knowing where you are going helps prevent writer's block. It also allows a writer to skip to another chapter out of order if he is experiencing trouble with a given chapter.

Despite the detail included in chapter outlines, they should be regarded merely as reference guides while writing and editing the first draft. Writers should always feel free to let their creative juices flow and take the story in a different direction. Being totally tied to an outline risks destroying the creative energy that makes writing such an enormously satisfying experience. When a writer takes the story off-outline, he should wait a few days, go back and read the off-outline scene and ask himself if that really is the direction he wants to go. If it is, and often it will be, then just go back and change whatever summaries in the chapter outline that may require modification.

Example of a Chapter Outline – *The Litigators* (first three chapters)

1. **January 15, 2000. Ruth and George Bergstrom are rock solid, middle class people, deeply in love and devoted to their family. They live next door to an abandoned gas station. Not feeling well, Ruth arises early. As she goes outside to retrieve the morning newspaper, she suddenly experiences a neurological attack that leaves her partially paralyzed and unable to get back inside. George arises a little later and finds her half-frozen body on the front steps. He takes her to the hospital where her attack subsides almost as quickly as it appeared. Despite her naively stoic disposition, Ruth's doctor is quite concerned both by the severity of this attack and because this was the second of its kind in recent weeks. He asks Ruth about their previous office visit where she had informed him about the fact that there was a leaking underground storage tank at the gas station next door and that, for the last six months, there had been a company out at the site pumping something into the ground around the gas station. George explained that just a few days ago, as Dr. McIntosh had suggested earlier, Ruth wrote a letter to the company asking for information about any environmental hazards at the site.**

2. **January 15, 2000. Boyd Campbell is an athletic and enthusiastic university professor who recently left the security of academia to form his own company. EnviroClean is a biotechnology company that uses a genetically engineered microbe, P-27, to clean up hazardous waste spills, including leaking underground gasoline tanks from filling stations. He is married to Kathleen Campbell, a medical doctor. They are both as**

excited about their careers as the Bergstroms are about their family, but they are also very community spirited and deeply sensitive people. During an early morning run around a local lake on a bitter cold winter morning, Campbell hears the sirens heading for the Bergstrom's home and wonders to himself what might be wrong. That day is a special one in the life of EnviroClean, as Campbell is meeting with his lawyers and investment bankers to plan a public offering of stock to finance the fast growth of his budding young company. It is also the day a letter of inquiry arrives from Ruth Little about EnviroClean's project at the gas station next door.

3. Campbell meets investment bankers and his attorney, Henry Holton, at Holton's private club. In attendance also is Allison Forbes, Holton's bright and sassy protégé in Holton's law firm, Darby and Witherspoon, Minneapolis' largest and most prestigious law firm. The investment bankers are enthusiastic about investing in EnviroClean, but Campbell naively makes reference to the letter from Ruth Little, prompting curious inquiries. After the luncheon, Holton, Forbes, and Campbell meet privately at the law office to discuss the letter. Holton fears the possibility of spurious litigation with catastrophic consequences for the public offering and insists on a tough, almost threatening responsive letter signed personally by him as senior partner of the firm. Forbes and Campbell are both concerned with this hard-nosed approach but Campbell eventually accedes to Holton's advice. Passing reference is made by Holton to the favorable business climate in Bermuda for high tech companies.

A WORD ABOUT TIME MANAGEMENT

Most of my students who are working on first novels and memoires also have jobs, families, and community activities. They are enormously busy. So how do they find time to write a novel, a challenging and labor-intensive project? Well, some don't. Their books linger year after year with only modest progress. Many of them attend writer's classes, which I gladly offer them, writer's workshops, and writers' groups hoping for ideas that will add value to their creative writing projects. What they don't do regularly is write.

The difference between writers who move their projects along at a productive pace and those that flounder is not, I repeat, not that the productive writers have fewer other commitments than the less productive group. Almost everyone who is bright enough to write a novel has a busy life. Bright people are generally engaged professionally, socially and civically. The real difference is that the productive group plans their schedules wisely, carving out and reserving time for writing whereas the unproductive group allows time for writing only when their calendars are free of other activities.

The message is clear – if you're serious about writing and really want to complete your project, you will schedule time on your calendar for writing just as you do for every other activity. Although I encourage my students to devote as much time as possible, the most important goal is to schedule at least some time every week and write that time down on the calendar. Once it's on the calendar, guard that commitment as you would guard any other commitment. If a friend calls for coffee at Starbucks, you're busy, end of story.

Everyone will develop different schedules for writing, and everyone will have differing amounts of time available for writing. Find a routine that works for you -- two mornings a week, two evenings a week, every Saturday without fail, 4 p.m. to 6 p.m. three days a week, a week of vacation time from work devoted to writing. Maybe every week will have to be different. If so, set a day, perhaps Sunday, where you calendar your writing time for the following week. Agree with yourself on the amount of time you can devote to writing, and then establish any pattern you can live with and stick to it.

A busy schedule does not make writing a novel or short story impossible; it requires planning. The people who tend to plan the best are the people who are already very busy. The worst planners paradoxically tend to be people who have very little on their agendas. So, regardless of whether you lead a hectic or a leisurely life, adopting a well-conceived schedule for completing your writing project is essential.

CHAPTER 10

How to Use Verbs to Create a Powerful Story

Verb selection is perhaps the most important tool that writers leave in their war chests. We writers often spend our precious time searching the far recesses of our brains and our thesauruses to find just the perfect word to describe some character or event. We are generally wasting our time, which should be spent searching for the right verb instead of the right adjective or adverb.

Using adjectives alone to describe a character is like driving a railroad spike with a tack hammer; it's really easy to swing the hammer but it does very little to advance the spike. Adjectives are not high performers. They do not bring nouns to life, and the poor noun is relegated to wiling away its time as a couch potato until some verb shows up and prods it into action. Adjectives add a bit of color to the story, but the story is more effectively delivered by verbs.

But, as I often tell my students, not all verbs are alike. There are those that I like to call vanilla bland verbs, and those that I call emotive verbs. The differences between them are enormous.

VANILLA BLAND VERBS

We all know that verbs are action words. They force nouns to do something, be it physical or mental. This is the unique essence of all verbs. Verbs that accomplish this, and only this basic purpose are Vanilla Bland Verbs. They create action, but they tell us nothing about the nature of the action or the state of mind of the actor. Vanilla bland verbs are motion without emotion.

EMOTIVE VERBS

Many verbs actually serve two purposes. They stimulate some activity, but they also reveal important information about the nature of the action as well as the state of mind of the actor. I call these Emotive Verbs. Emotive verbs are the knights of the writer's kingdom, and it is these verbs, not adjectives or adverbs, that writers should spend their time searching for.

I have a favorite ice cream shop I visit, as often as my belt buckle allows, and in nineteen years of frequent sojourns I have never seen anyone order plain vanilla ice cream, at least not without a brownie base or a selection of toppings. OK, that's a weak analogy, I agree, but the point is a good one nonetheless; people like rich flavor in their sweet treats, and they like it even more in their reading material.

Let's check out some simple examples to see what I mean.

"He walked into the room."
In the context of this sentence, "walk" is a vanilla bland verb because it stimulates action without saying anything at all about the individual or his emotional state as he entered the room. In fact, it's really quite pointless even to write this sentence because it conveys no useful information to the reader. If the scene that follows this sentence takes place in a room, the reader can readily infer that, unless the individual is Santa Claus, he must have walked into the room. So why bother giving this useless information to the reader? Why not just begin the scene in the room?

Perhaps, you say, it *is* important to tell the reader how our character entered the room because his emotional state at the time may be useful in setting the tone for the scene. If so, the writer has two options, use adjectives or adverbs to set the emotional tone of the scene, or use emotive verbs to accomplish the same thing. Let's extend my example of "walking into a room" to compare the use of emotive verbs with adjectives/adverbs to describe several possible ways in which our hypothetical character may have entered the room.

Emotive Verbs	Descriptive Adjectives/adverbs
He barged into the room.	He walked into the room, angry and upset.
He strode into the room.	He confidently walked into the room.
He sashayed into the room.	He walked into the room, cocky and aloof.
He skipped into the room.	He walked into the room, happy as a lark.
He shuffled into the room.	He walked into the room, depressed and despondent.
He stomped into the room.	He rudely walked into the room.
He stumbled into the room.	He walked into the room, drunk as usual.
He flew into the room.	He walked into the room, anxiety painted all over his face.

Which column of sentences better captures the emotions of the person entering the room? Is there any doubt that the use of emotive verbs is more descriptive than describing the same emotions with adjectives and adverbs? Clearly, even when vanilla bland verbs are combined with adjectives and adverbs the quality of the image still suffers. I would argue, for example, that a man who "walks" into a room cannot possibly be as angry as one who "barges" into the room. And a woman who "walks" into a room cannot be as despondent as one who "shuffles" into the room. And so forth. It is the verb that sets the scene, not the adjective.

In some cases, you may feel tempted to do double duty, combine emotive verbs with other descriptors. For example, you may feel tempted to say, "He barged into the room, angry and upset." I do not favor this approach because I like to give the reader credit for being reasonably perceptive. Readers do not need to be told that a character is angry if they are first told that the character barged into the room. They are fully capable of making their own judgments about the character's state of mind based on the verb used to describe the mode of entry.

There is another reason why emotive verbs are better descriptors than adjectives and adverbs — emotive verbs "show" whereas adjectives and adverbs "tell." The sentence "He walked into the room, angry and upset" is really just the writer's personal opinion of the character's state of mind. But readers do not care about the writer's opinion. Readers want to make their own interpretations of characters' emotions based on what happens in the scene. The writer may hope that the reader interprets his use of the verb "barged" to indicate anger, but the reader gets to make that call. Maybe, for instance, as the scene unfolds, the reader concludes that the character is just rude rather than angry. He has every right to make that call, even if the writer disagrees. The writer's job is to pick the verb that best depicts the emotion or state of mind he wants to create; the reader's job is to interpret the emotion as he sees fit.

Let's look at a few more examples.

Example 1A

"She walked down the hallway and entered his office."

Example 1B

"She crept down the hallway and quietly slipped through the doorway into his office."

Example 1C

"She skipped down the hallway and bounded into his office."

The problem with Example 1A is that "walk" and "enter" provide little information about the woman and her emotional state. These words do nothing more than move her through a hallway and into an office. Who cares about that? If it's important enough to tell the reader about her movements in the hallway, then you should also tell the reader how she moved, how she felt, and what were her emotions as she approached the office. That's what the reader really wants to know. Examples 1B and 1C are far superior because they help create the tone of the scene and infer important information about the woman's emotions. In 1B, the verbs tell the reader that she is cautious, nervous, and reticent and imply a sense of foreboding. In 1C, the verbs tell the reader that she is young, vivacious, and happy, and imply a sense of excitement.

Example 2A

"Joe went to his office."

Example 2B

"Joe drove like a maniac to make it to his office by precisely 7:00."

Example 2C

"Joe streamed his favorite Rachmaninoff as he made the leisurely drive to his office one last time."

Example 2A is wasted energy, wasted words. It's totally unimportant that Joe "went" to his office, so much so that the scene could begin at the office instead of in Joe's car. But, if the drive is important to you as a writer, there must be a reason it's important, and that reason is what the reader wants to know. In examples 2B and 2C, the reason why the trip to the office is important is that it captures Joe's emotional state at the time he arrives – quite tense in 2B and extremely relaxed in 2C. Bottom line, never write paragraph 2A, or anything like it; choose either paragraph 2B or 2C instead.

Example 3A

> **"Kate had a perfect plan in mind."**

Example 3B

> **"Kate spent the entire night devising the perfect plan."**

Example 3C

> **"A clever idea sprung spontaneously out of nowhere as Kate lounged in the tranquil privacy of her hot tub."**

Example 3A is weak because the verb "had" provides no information about Kate. The reader would much prefer examples 3B or 3C because they offer valuable inferences about Kate's emotional state as her plan unfurled.

Example 4

> **"Sarah was on the train for two hours."**

This sentence is so obviously vanilla bland that it's not even worthy of providing alternatives. The verb "to be" means nothing more than "to exist," which provides the reader no information that he does not already know. If Sarah is on the train, she must exist. The only detail the reader might care about is why Sarah was on the train, where she was going, and what her emotional state was during her ride. The verb "to be" does not provide this information.

The bottom line: choose your verbs carefully; select only

those verbs that fully capture the nature of the action and, more importantly, the emotional state of the actor.

Unfortunately, there are hundreds of vanilla bland verbs that fail us as writers because they merely describe some rote mechanical action without providing any real insight into the nature of the action. And, not surprisingly, these are the very verbs that dominate much of our daily conversations. I cannot list all vanilla bland verbs here, but I will give you a few examples of the many verbs that are vanilla bland in most contexts.

Come, came
Do, did
Drive, drove
Eat, ate
Enter, entered
Get, got
Go, went
Has, had
Is, was
Move, moved
Place, placed
Put, put
Stand, stood
Say, said (except in citing dialogue)
See, saw
Sit, sat
Walk, walked

There are dozens more examples of vanilla bland verbs. Be on the lookout for them and avoid them wherever possible.

VERB TENSES – SIMPLE IS BETTER

A related issue to verb choice is verb tense choice. The English language contains, by my count at least, seventeen separate verb tenses. For you grammarians, here's my list:

> Simple present, present progressive, simple past, past progressive, simple present perfect, present perfect progressive, simple past perfect, past perfect progressive, future, future-going to, future progressive, future perfect simple, conditional simple, conditional progressive, conditional perfect, conditional perfect progressive.

(Some grammarians hotly debate the definition of, and therefore the number of tenses, but this is my book, so I go with my number.)

Now that you know the answer to an otherwise obtuse Trivia question, I ask you to forget about all but two of these tenses – simple present, and simple past. Simple is better; complex is worse. It's not grammatically worse, but it's almost invariably literarily worse. And the reason is, yes, simple; complex verb tenses are often quite distracting.

Here's an example of what I mean.

"He had been going to do something about it."

Versus

"He planned to do something about it."

What really does it mean that "he had been going to do something about it"? While the sentence is grammatically correct, why not just say, "He planned to do something about it"? Complex verb tenses take the focus off the otherwise powerful language you have worked so hard to create for the reader's entertainment and admiration.

In my opinion, 90% of the verbs in most literary fiction ought be either simple present or simple past tense. All the reader really needs to know is whether the action is ongoing or whether it occurred previously. The real focus should be on the nature of the action and its impact on the characters.

Not only is the limiting of verb tenses a wise literary strategy, it is also the easiest way to write. I often see manuscripts with multiple, inconsistent tenses in the same paragraph, sometimes even in the same sentence. If you use only a single tense most of the time, this grammatical misstep is readily avoided.

GERUNDS AND PARTICIPLES

Gerunds are nouns created by adding "ing" to the end of a verb, e.g., swimming. I have no objection to the use of gerunds; in fact, many (like "swimming") constitute the only real choice a writer has.

Participles are verbs that function as an adverb or adjective. In the present tense participles often end in "ing" just like gerunds. An example is "finishing touches." The word "finishing" is a participle. Again, I have no objection to this use of participles.

DANGLING PARTICIPLES

The big problem with participles is the tendency that most people and many writers have to use dangling participles. A dangling participle occurs when a sentence begins or ends with a participle that doesn't modify the subject to which it refers. Here are two examples.

Example 1

"We reached the top of the hill and saw the river, feeling totally elated."

"Feeling" is a dangling participle since it does not modify river;

that is, it is "we," not the river, who feels elated. The correct way to write this sentence is "We felt totally elated when we reached the top of the hill and saw the falls."

Example 2

"Climbing the hill, the river came in view."

"Climbing" is a dangling participle since it doesn't modify "river." The correct way to write this sentence is "Climbing the hill, we saw the river come into view" or "We saw the river come into view as we neared the top of the hill." In the first option, placing the participle at the beginning is correct because it now modifies "we" rather than "river."

Dangling participles are very weak sentence structures, and they also stick out like a sore thumb with literary agents and publishers who may review your work. Even when they do not dangle, clauses beginning with a participle tend to produce weak sentences. Make an effort to avoid them entirely, even if you use them correctly.

This is about the only grammar lesson I'm going to give in this book. I give it because, in my experience as a writing instructor and coach, it is one of the more common and least understood grammatical errors that I see in the manuscripts of budding authors.

CHAPTER 11

How to Use Simile, Metaphor, and Side Scenes to Paint Compelling Characters

Now that we understand the importance of emotive verbs in adding color to written images, let's focus on several other techniques that also contribute enormously to the power of your writing and the development of your characters.

SIMILES

Technically a simile is any comparison that uses the words "like" or "as." Sly as a fox, hard like a rock, quick as a wink, wise as an owl, dumb as a fence post, slow as a snail, happy as a clam. These are all good examples of similes. (Just don't use any of them yourself because they are all trite and overworked.)

The advantage of similes is that a character or object can be described through the use of an image that is easily understood by the reader. A writer's job is, first and foremost, to paint images that evoke emotion, suspense, mystery, and compelling characters, and similes are ready-made for the job. Adjectives can be very colorful and descriptive, but they are not images and do not automatically paint a word picture of the scene the writer seeks to depict. Compare, for example, the following.

Example 1

"Sara was furious almost beyond belief."

Example 2

"Sara was as rabid as a grizzly sow separated from her cub."

No matter how hard I try to find just the right adjective to portray the extent of Sara's wrath, I will almost invariably find a simile that does the job better. In Example 2, the reader fully understands the enormous fury of a female bear whose cub is threatened and easily transposes that image to the character. The adjective "furious" even when accentuated with the modifier "almost beyond belief" falls dismally short by comparison.

Exactly how do writers find good similes? The first step is to verbalize the characteristic or emotion one seeks to portray. In the example above, the emotion was anger. Once writers choose the emotion or characteristic they seek to portray, the next step is to search their memory bank for vivid examples of that emotion. We must let our imagination run wild. If it's an object we seek to describe, one possibility is to search for ways to personify that object. For example,

"The sun peaked through the clouds like a mischievous child in a game of hide-and-seek."

By personifying an inanimate object like the sun, we give that object the characteristics of the humanoid figure we describe. Here we paint a picture of the sun as an impish, child-like character, an image that portends a happy, perhaps frolicsome day ahead. Such an image is very difficult to paint with adjectives alone.

The converse is also true; if you want to describe a human, look for inanimate objects, animals, and other creatures for sources of comparison. For example,

"Sheila was as focused as a gecko perched a tongue-shot away from its prey."

By comparing Sheila with a gecko, I give her the gecko's characteristic of intense patience as it waits for its prey to slip just a millimeter closer. Adjectives cannot accomplish this.

Let's try one more example, the emotion "happiness." The same rules apply. Look for some memory of extreme happiness in your life; imagine some event that would produce enormous happiness for you or someone close to you; or just let your imagination run wild until you find the perfect image of happiness. Here's what I found after only a few minutes of imagination time.

"Sarah was as happy as a mother breasting her child at the moment of birth."

Adjectives are useless for painting an image of happiness even remotely equivalent to the image of happiness evoked by this or other equally descriptive similes.

METAPHORS

A metaphor is a simile without the "as" or "like."

"The guy's a real snake."
"What a turkey!"
"The cop stared him down with laser eyes."
"He's a wolf in sheep's clothing."

These are metaphors because, while none of these statements is literally true, they all conjure up a vivid image that is quickly transferred to the character in question. Metaphors are not used as frequently as similes, but, when appropriate, they can be even more powerful descriptors. For example,

"Joe's business was a runaway truck on the downside of a mountain."
Translation: Joe's business was on a fast decline.

"That old oak tree was a mute historian to generations of human suffering at end of its limbs."
Translation: many slaves had been lynched on the oak tree.

"The fullback was a mad rhino with an insatiable thirst for blood, my blood."
Translation: I was scared to death the fullback would run my way.

The benefit of a metaphor is that it is more powerful to say that a character is a mad rhino than to say he is *like* a mad rhino. The risk of metaphors is loss of credibility for overstating the analogy. Readers want to see amazing characters, even those that are almost unbelievable. I said "almost." There must be at least a reasonable claim that a character of the writer's imagination could possibly exist. Telling a reader that a fullback is like a mad rhino is one thing but telling the reader that the fullback is a mad rhino is quite another. Actually, I think readers of that sentence will forgive me my bold-faced lie and easily understand that I am only exaggerating the fullback's physical prowess and will not challenge the assertion. If I'm right, then there is benefit to the use of metaphor rather than simile.

SIDE SCENES

I use the term "side scene" to refer to a scene, usually a very brief one, whose sole purpose is to advance the development of a character who is important to the main plot. By definition, a side scene is irrelevant to the plot or storyline and does not even indirectly advance the plot. It is useful only because it provides important information about a significant character. Side scenes should almost always be short in order to avoid distracting the reader from the actual storyline or plot.

Let me give you an example. Suppose a writer wants to describe a given character as "despicable." He might use a verb, simile, or metaphor to do the job, but he could also create a brief side scene. Consider the following examples.

Example 1:

"Derek was a despicable human being."

Example 2:

In his senior year in high school, Derek poured a bucket of cow manure in the locker of a girl who refused a date with him.
This dastardly deed obviously has nothing to do with the story line, but who cares? The sentence, while not furthering the plot, clearly paints a lurid image of a despicable human being, and it does so far more convincingly than simply using the adjective "despicable." And, because the side scene is very short, the reader gets the benefit of a colorful image without risk of distraction. Just one more tool in the writer's war chest for painting compelling pictures in words.

A side scene can be longer than a single sentence without distracting the reader. As a broad guideline, I recommend limiting side scenes to one paragraph, although occasionally I have seen side scenes of a page or two used very effectively. Here's an example.

Example 1:

Martin was a scoundrel and a free-loader."

Example 2:

"Years before, Martin arranged to be introduced to the daughter of the president of MedOptical, a major supplier of ophthalmological equipment throughout the United States. It was a hot and heavy affair for several years, fancy parties, yachts, the whole deal. Then one day the FDA forced the company to discontinue and recall its best product. Six months later MedOptical went belly up. That was the day Martin dumped her. Just like that and it was all over."

Short side scenes like this soliloquy can be helpful in painting vivid pictures of important characters. Merely writing that "Martin was a scoundrel and free-loader" is a weak and rather unconvincing observation by the author. A brief side scene of an incident in Martin's past provides a far more convincing image of the odious nature of the man.

CHAPTER 12

How to Use Dialogue to Create Compelling Characters

D ialogue constitutes a direct connection between the speaker and his brain. Short of using an omniscient narrator (which almost always is a bad idea), dialogue is the only way to know what any given character is actually thinking. Thus, the importance of dialogue in character development cannot be overestimated.

Dialogue has another advantage. Unlike narrative, dialogue always occurs onstage, front and center, in full view of the reader. Narrative is listening to the story; dialogue is watching the story through the mouths of the characters. Readers always want to be there in person, to feel a part of the action, and dialogue always makes this happen.

Dialogue can also be utilized to create tension and conflict far easier than narrative. Talk between characters can be very harsh, combative and confrontational. Adversarial dialogue is effective in painting a vivid image of the speakers and, in only a few words, peak the readers emotional involvement with the story.

Dialogue should be short and sweet and must serve some mission important to the plot line. Every word must count. Pointless chatter, however clever the writer may think it is, must be discarded. Similarly, never insert dialogue simply to provide information to the reader; this task is better accomplished through narrative.

To evaluate the quality of any given passage of dialogue, ask yourself these questions.

- Does the dialogue introduce or aggravate tension or conflict?
- Does the dialogue introduce or heighten mystery or suspense?
- Does the dialogue portray the speaker as a compelling character?
- Does the dialogue advance the plot?
- Does the dialogue take the reader into the emotional state of mind of the speaker?

A useful technique for creating conflict in dialogue is to assign different perspectives to the speakers. Indeed, I would argue, if the characters do not have different perspectives, the dialogue is probably not worth including. We are not writing cocktail party conversations filled with aimless chatter where everyone nods in agreement between sips of wine. We are developing characters through conflict and emotion, two elements that are invariably missing from cocktail party conversation absent some attendee's overindulgence. The speakers' motives and goals should be different, or, better yet, inconsistent, like two people speaking on different wavelengths each one destined never to hear the other.

Example:

"**Did you get my text yesterday?**"
"**What text? Did you bring my book back?**"
"**I sent you a text at 8:34 yesterday, check your phone.**"
"**My phone never dinged; it always dings twice when I get a text. Where's my book?**"

This over simplified example illustrates a good technique for using dialogue to create conflict between the characters. Each character has his own agenda and each agenda is inconsistent with the other. While my example portrays only a trivial dispute about a text and a book, when the inconsistency focuses on a significant element of the plot, the dialogue can be very useful in bringing out each of the character's differing personas.

Writing dialogue is not easy, but here are a few simple points to keep in mind.

1. Consistency.

The speech must be consistent with the character's background, education, ethnicity, culture, age, social station, and intelligence. This is not as easy as it seems. We writers are who we are and our tendency is to write words we would speak. If we do that, all our characters will run around sounding just like the author, a sure route to failure. I encourage all first-time novelists to prepare character profiles (See Chapter 9) outlining the backgrounds of all characters to use as a reference when writing dialogue for any given character. I often have some real or imaginary person in mind when I write dialogue so I have a mental picture of my character. I find this helpful in assuring that my speech patterns differ between one character and another.

2. Grammar.

People do not speak in grammatically correct sentences, not even highly educated people. A number of years ago during the height of my legal career as a trial lawyer, I presented what I thought was a brilliant final argument to the jury. I was so impressed with myself that I asked the court reporter to transcribe my speech to use as a training tool for young lawyers at my firm. A few weeks later the transcript found its way to my desk. It was god-awful! My grammar was terrible; my sentences were frequently incomplete. Several times I even interrupted a point

I was making in mid-sentence and inexplicably moved on to an unrelated point in the same sentence. I was repetitious. I was, by any red-blooded English teacher's definition of the term, virtually illiterate. Needless to say, I never showed that transcript to another human being. But, as poorly spoken as it was, the speech was in fact excellent oratory. It carried the day for my client, and we won a very difficult major trial.

You get the point. If we write elegant oratory for our characters, we will be creating people who do not exist. The only truly great speeches are those that are carefully written in advance, often with several edits and redrafting, and then read word for word to the audience, often with the aid of a teleprompter.

3. Completeness.

People interrupt each other all the time when they speak, especially if they are animated, as we all want our characters to be. We don't let each other finish our sentences, especially when we are in the midst of a hot exchange of views. Dialogue must mimic these real life conversations, especially during episodes of emotional conflict and tension.

4. Responsiveness.

People often do not directly answer each other's questions or respond to each other's comments. Most humans are much better talkers than we are listeners. Instead of directly responding to a point made, we often ignore the point our conversant makes and jump into the point we want to make. Our words just fly past each other's ears, particularly where we are in conflict with one another. At best, any response we are likely to give in moments of tension and drama tends to be oblique or circuitous.

5. Conflict and Emotion.

Dialogue is not about exchanging information between characters and passing it along to the reader. It is about developing characters through conflict and emotion.

Let's look at a few of examples of good dialogue, all taken from my novel, *The Litigators*.

Example 1 – A meeting between lawyer and client

"I don't know, Henry," Boyd replied, "Maybe it would be worthwhile sitting down with Dillon Love to see if the case might get resolved."

"Boyd, these plaintiff's lawyers are a contagious plague. Pay any one of these piranhas, and you'll have hundreds more nipping at your billfold until hell freezes over."

Campbell lost what color remained in his face. He looked at Allison and sagged in his chair.

Seeing this, Holten exploded. "We must go forward. We must do it aggressively, and we must win at all costs. It's either that, or you can give up all your dreams and go back to the university and teach zit-faced morons. Your entrepreneurial days will be over."

"I just can't believe that, Henry," Campbell said.

"You understand science, Boyd. I understand law. Trust me. We'll do right by you and your company."

This short dialogue accomplishes three important objectives.

1. It perpetuates an intractable conflict between lawyer and client, pitting them as combatants rather than collaborators. This is a major theme of the novel, where clients are forced to find justice, not through their lawyers but in spite of them.

2. Henry Holten is portrayed as an arrogant ass and Boyd Campbell as a meek and malleable professor. Both are compelling in their own right as the reader feels sympathy for Campbell and disdain for Holten. Remember, a character can be compelling by being an arrogant ass as much as by being a Mother Teresa.
3. Holten's admonition to "trust me" presages an uncertain outcome, thereby contributing to the ongoing mystery as to who will win the case.

Example 2 – A casual meeting between Henry Holten and his colleague Allison Forbes

"By the way," Alison asked, "what took you down to Bermuda?"

"Oh, nothing much," Holten replied. "We've got a client there, a small genetics company. I stop to see them once in a while, just an excuse to get back to Bermuda really."

This brief dialogue is another example of a side scene, a scene that does not advance the story but which is inserted for another purpose, here, to create mystery about what could possibly be going on in Bermuda and have some bearing on a lawsuit in Minnesota. Note also that Holton did not answer the question Forbes asked, a rather typical circumstance in our everyday conversations.

Example 3

Love said, "I'm prepared to raise the money I need to finance the case by taking out a second mortgage on our house."

"Don't do that to Laurie, Cindy pleaded. "Don't risk everything you and Laurie have made together for this one case. It's already been stressful on your marriage. It's just not worth it."

"My marriage is fine," Love said, "and it's none of your damned business anyway."

This brief dialogue is included for two purposes.

1. It adds to Dillon Love's characterization as a naïve and unyielding dreamer, a Don Quixote of sorts who battles on, entirely blind to reality.
2. It adds tension by introducing Love's marriage as one more obstacle that impedes his goal of winning his case at all costs. How will Love respond to a choice between his marriage and his case?

The bottom line: take time to write good dialogue. It's far more useful than narrative in building compelling characters. It's also a nice break for readers, because they get to turn pages faster.

CHAPTER 13

The All-Important First Page

The next time you are in your favorite bookstore, spend a few minutes watching customers browse through books before selecting one. Everyone looks at the title and the cover; most people look at a review or two on the back cover; and, if that has peaked their interest, they may read the first paragraph. That's it. Almost no one reads more than a single paragraph before deciding whether to buy the book.

If they do buy the book, it remains on probation, a very short probation. Most readers today are extremely impatient. They have dozens of good books recommended to them by friends and reviewers, and if the writer does not capture their attention quickly they are likely to put the book down and move on down their reading list.

The same is true for literary agents and publishers, both of whom are inundated with manuscripts vying for their attention. And because they reject most manuscripts they review, they begin each manuscript with skepticism. The writer must prove his/her worth without delay.

The message is clear – the first page is the most important page; the first paragraph is the most important paragraph, and the first sentence is the most important sentence. Don't mess around introducing your characters or their environs. Don't mess around setting up the plot. Don't try to self-justify any delay with the excuse that important information must first be communicated to the reader. Readers do not want information; they want arousal.

The goal of the first paragraph must be to excite the reader's curiosity and draw him into the story. But what, you say, are the tools a writer has to accomplish this goal? Here's my list.

1. Use the first paragraph to introduce a character that is both unique and fascinating, someone who would immediately cause you to do a double take if you passed him on the street. Would you turn your head for an individual who appeared normal in every respect? Normal people are who we all want to be, but they are not who we want to read about.

2. Insert an omen of harsh challenges to come, for example, death, incarceration, divorce, or loss of a loved one. This can often be accomplished with only a single word, carefully selected, one that stands out from the rest of the paragraph.

3. Create an immediate scene. By "immediate" I mean a scene that involves the reader, one that he can see, one that draws him into the action. "Immediacy" is not achieved by narrative summaries or descriptions, because narratives merely "tell" the reader something the author wants him to know. Readers do not want to be told anything; they want to be entertained, and entertainment comes from seeing the action first hand with their own eyes, not being told about the action by a narrator.

Let's look at a few examples.

Example 1: (From Franz Kafka's *Metamorphosis*)

"One morning, as Gregor Samsa was waking up from anxious dreams, he discovered that in bed he had been changed into a monstrous verminous bug."

This is one of the most famous first sentences ever written. The sentence has it all: it introduces a character who is destined to be fascinating; it introduces an ominous mystery that begs the reader to keep going; and it creates immediacy by taking the reader off his couch and forcing him into the middle of Samsa's horrible bedroom.

Example 2: (Potential first sentence for a murder mystery.)

As nighttime suffocated the last feeble rays of a December sun and the first of the cold winter winds battered the ancient timbers of the old prairie church I had served for nearly two decades, little did I know that the furious winter that was about to begin would see three men and a child die in this peaceful, sacred place.

I like this possible first sentence because it portends several unseemly murders inside a church, a most unique location for a murder mystery. The contrast between a peaceful, rural church and three awful murders immediately hooks the reader who desperately wants to know the whos and whys about such unusual crimes. Likewise, the choice of the minister as the narrator of a murder mystery occurring at his own church is a bit tantalizing and asks the reader to speculate about what role the minister actually plays. In short, the reader is immediately brought into the story and does not want to leave.

Example 3: (Potential first sentence for a novel about a young girl who somehow pulls herself out of poverty and family dysfunction to become a famous physician.)

As Samantha kneeled on the ground and stroked the bloodied dreadlocks of her best friend and felt her last weak puff of air against her cheek, her mother leaned from a second-floor window of the projects across the street and yelled, "git your sorry ass in here, girl; she ain't none of your business now."

This possible first sentence does a nice job introducing the enormous obstacles that have been thrust upon the young and compassionate Samantha: obvious poverty, family dysfunction, and a heartless mother. The reader does not yet know where Samatha is headed, but he absolutely is empathetic and desperately wants to know how Samantha will cope with her extremely challenging circumstances. In short, the reader is hooked in only a single sentence.

CHAPTER 14

Point of View

Who's going to tell the story? Or, to ask the same question differently, in which character do you want the reader to inhabit? Does it have to be the same person throughout the book? How do I decide?

Point of view refers to the individual who has personal knowledge of the events that make up the story. It can be anyone, an individual writing a memoir, an objective narrator who has acquired information about the events in the story from some known or unknown source, or an omniscient narrator who knows everything, including this story.

Deciding who to tell the story is an important decision. The challenging task of arousing the emotions of the reader and drawing him into the story is the responsibility of the narrator. Whichever choice is made, it is inevitable that the story will be dramatically affected, and the reader's experience will be significantly altered. Usually the point of view is consistent throughout the book, and this is what I recommend for previously unpublished writers. It is technically feasible, however, to use more than one narrator if caution is exercised to avoid confusing the reader.

Whoever is selected to be narrator, he or she must have personal knowledge of the events that the story portrays. Any one person, for example, cannot know what is going on in someone else's brain, just as someone who was born in 1995 cannot have personal knowledge of what may have happened in 1960. These issues often affect the choice of narrator as much as strategic dramatic considerations, although there are a number of ways to get around these problems. Although, for example, I cannot know what is going on in your brain, you can tell me and thereby give me the personal knowledge that enables me to report what you said (although of course you might have been lying or confused). Similarly, a narrator born in 1995 can gain personal knowledge of events that preceded his birth in a variety of ways: through dialogue with an older person, from old diaries or personal journals, from newspaper articles, from public records, or from inference based on a series of known facts.

Let's look at the options.

FIRST PERSON NARRATION

The story is told in the first person, usually by one of the major characters in the book. I favor using the first person in memoirs, because the reader really wants to hear the story from the person who is the focus of the book. But first person can be used in any story, and it does not have to be a major character. A minor character that is close to the action and has a relationship with most of the characters in the story can serve as a first-person narrator. This can sometimes be effective because minor characters generally have no skin in the game, tend to be viewed as credible reporters, and are able to offer neutral observations about the major characters.

The first-person narrator does not even have to be alive, and a deceased person can theoretically tell his own story. It can even be a dog or other pet, or an old house, although I would not recommend any of these options to the novice writer.

So, what are the pros and cons of first-person narration?

Pros

1. First-person can be very powerful, because the writer has open access to the inner thoughts and emotions of the storyteller. This is helpful in portraying characters that are very bright or very complex.
2. Some factual details that cannot be known by a third-person narrator are available in the first-person.
3. With first person narration, an eyewitness is always telling the action, so the story is credible, on stage and in the moment.

Cons

1. The writer loses his ability to relate some facts that cannot be known by the first-person narrator. This can be problematic when some of the action takes place outside the presence of the first-person narrator, as, for example, when there are multiple major characters or stories that take place over long periods of time and distant locations. There are solutions to this problem if first person narration is important, but it is a problem the writer must find a way to address.
2. There is a high risk of the author slipping into "telling" instead of "showing." When the writer has immediate access to the narrator's inner thoughts, the temptation to blurt it all out can be overpowering. If the temptation is not constantly monitored and avoided, the likelihood of failure is high.
3. There is a tendency for characters describing themselves to be viewed as egotistical and lose credibility as a neutral observer.
4. Writers must be vigilant to avoid starting too many sentences with the word "I." The tendency for first person

narrators to use the word "I" is ever present, but it is also easily avoided if the writer is alert to it; first person narrators are perfectly capable of telling their stories based on their observations of events without overusing the word "I."

THIRD PERSON – OBJECTIVE NARRATORS

Third person is the most common choice for popular fiction and commercial bestsellers. It is also the easiest form of narration to write and, except for memoirs, the preferred choice for most aspiring authors. The ideal third person narrator is the character with the biggest obstacles to overcome, the most to win or lose, because that is generally the strongest and most intense way of telling the story. However, a third parson narrator can also be an independent observer, someone who witnesses the actions from outside and relays what he sees to the reader.

With third person narration, the story can be told either from the point of view of a single outside individual who observes the action but who plays no role in the story itself, or from the point of view of one or more of the actual characters. Multiple characters can also tell the story, in third person, one character at a time. In that case, the point of view falls to the character on stage at any given moment as he or she relates what they see and do while they are on stage. That is to say, a given character may narrate the story in one chapter but not even present in another, where the narration duties fall to a different character, but still in the third person.

Pros

1. This is the easiest form of narration to write.
2. Readers appreciate the third person. The story is told just like the old campfire tales that we all love to remember from our childhoods.

3. It's very flexible in that it effectively allows the writer to change point of view from one chapter to another as the narrator relates events particular to each character.

Cons

1. The credibility of the narrator may become a concern. Objective narrators may possess great knowledge about the events that have taken place, but he cannot know everything. We accept detailed facts related in the first person, but we may question the authenticity of details that a third person narrator tells us. How does he know that?

2. Objective narrators do not know what goes on in anyone's head. The only way the writer can get into a character's head is to create a dialogue in which that character says what he is thinking. Of course, the reader may believe that the character does not have the impartiality to assess his own thoughts accurately or that the character may be lying.

THIRD-PERSON – OMNISCIENT NARRATORS

Stories can also be told by omniscient narrators. Omniscient narrators are third parties that know everything, even what's going on inside the head of any given character. In reality, an omniscient narrator is actually the author himself. This is the easiest way to write, because the author never has to worry about the narrator having insufficient personal knowledge of an event to tell the story. Unfortunately, it almost invariably produces very shallow characters because their true nature is revealed by a narrator/ author who tends to intrude into the characters' lives rather than allow the characters to tell their own story.

Pros

1. Omniscient narrators have all the same advantages of objective narrators.
2. Omniscient narrators also allow the writer to tell the story, because in truth they *are* the writer.
3. Omniscient narrators know what's going on in the minds of all characters so there is no detail beyond their personal knowledge.

Cons

- The temptation to tell versus show is extreme and hard to avoid. Because an omniscient narrator has access to everyone's brains, he tends to relate the thoughts and emotions he sees rather than go to all the trouble to write a scene that portrays those inner thoughts and emotions. Readers will not be happy. Nor will literary agents and publishers.
- Most publishers are leery of omniscient narrators. This factor alone should discourage most budding authors.

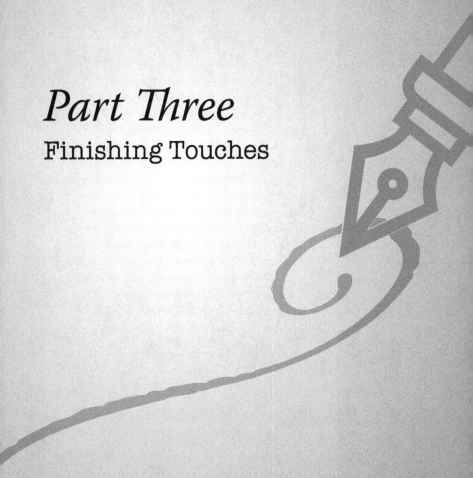

Part Three

Finishing Touches

CHAPTER 15

Writer's Block

As I mentioned earlier, Earnest Hemmingway believed that "The first draft is always shit." If Hemmingway initially wrote "shit," all the rest of us mere mortals are more than capable of doing the same. None of us, however, should follow Hemmingway's example and be so harshly critical of ourselves, certainly not during the creative writing phase. Hemmingway's own self-doubts apparently did not serve him well, as he committed suicide at the age of 61. Harsh self-criticism is counterproductive. I counsel all my students against being critical of their own writing during the creative writing phase. Critiques are reserved for the editing phase. Unfortunately, however easy it is to verbalize a positive attitude, every writer sooner or later questions his own abilities. This negativity is one of the main causes of writer's block.

A second cause is pumping dry one's well of creative ideas. This occurs when the writer becomes structurally confused about how exactly to put the story together, or he can't find what he believes are the perfect words or similes, or he can't figure out how to develop his characters into more compelling people. I outline below several recommendations for extricating oneself from writer's block once it occurs, but our real objective as writers is to avoid writer's block in the first place. So, let's start with prevention.

HOW TO AVOID WRITERS' BLOCK

1. Plan ahead. A good chapter outline allows you to sit down at your computer with ideas already in mind, so you don't just stare blankly at the screen, waste time and question your abilities.
2. Think of ideas and scenes while you are walking, running, biking, driving, or exercising so that you already have a few ideas in mind when you sit down to write. It's even a good idea to figure out what will be the first sentence you write when you get back to work. Avoid turning on your computer without knowing at least in a general sense the first words you will write, the first scene you will create.
3. Do not be judgmental about your writing while you are writing; you must let yourself go with the flow, let the words spill out onto the page. Judging is reserved for the editing process.
4. Never let negative thoughts creep into your mind while writing. You must believe in yourself, believe what you are writing has great promise. Enthusiasm for one's writing project provides enormous benefit and without any doubt stimulates creative, quality writing and reduces the risk of writer's block.

HOW TO OVERCOME WRITER'S BLOCK

There are a number of proven strategies to employ if you find yourself frustrated and depressed with your writing. Here's my list.

1. Write anything that comes into your mind, even if it's terrible. The mere act of writing, even if you don't like it, often generates good new ideas. Sometimes I force myself to write sentences that I know are terrible and will be deleted shortly, because almost invariably once any words

start flowing off my keyboard, good words generally follow soon thereafter.

2. Don't worry about picking the perfect word, the winning metaphor, the ideal adjective, and don't worry about grammar or spelling. When you've got good ideas, let them surge onto the page; it's easy to go back later and alter words, metaphors, and sentence structure.

3. Don't feel obligated to follow the outline you have prepared; let your creativity take the story wherever it goes; then change the outline to reflect the new direction of your story after you have let your off-outline text sit for a few days.

4. Go where your energy takes you. If you're having trouble with any given scene, skip ahead to another scene later in the book. Work on a scene that really excites you, one that will get your creative juices flowing again. Then go back and finish the earlier troublesome scene on another day. In my own case, I rarely write chapters in chronological order. I skip all over the place and pick scenes or chapters that happen to catch my fancy at the moment, scenes that I am really excited about writing. This is easy to do if you utilize chapter outlines.

5. Take a break and do something physical or athletic. Physical exertion is good for the brain and will often help you see through whatever problem has you presently confounded.

Because writers' block happens to every author in every book, you can't trust your own negative thoughts. Get over it!

CHAPTER 16

Editing

I think of fiction writing as a two-part process: the creative writing phase and the editing phase. Each phase requires an entirely different mentality and approach.

THE CREATIVE WRITING PHASE

During the creative writing phase one should allow the creative juices to flow freely, unencumbered by distracting side trips to a thesaurus, tedious searches of the deep recesses of our memories for the perfect simile, and over-concern about grammar, punctuation and typographical errors. Leave all those details for the editing phase. During the creative phase, a fiction writer should absolutely never doubt himself or criticize his own writing. We writers must believe that our writing is brilliant and that a National Book Award is just around the corner. Only by being positive and enthusiastic about one's work can a writer generate the creative energy required for good fiction.

THE EDITING PHASE

The exact opposite is true during the editing phase, where we force ourselves to be harshly critical of what we have written. Go into the editing phase as a highly suspicious perfectionist who cannot tolerate mediocrity. Think of yourself as a skeptical editor, someone who rejects nine out of every ten books he reads, and look at the book from his perspective. Only by fairly and impartially assessing our own work can we expect to uncover all the problems we have created and figure out a way to fix them.

I do not mean to suggest that editing is a form of masochistic self-torture. Far from it, editing, as I use the term, is a highly creative enterprise. It's an opportunity for writers to take what they have written to a new level. For me, the editing phase is a most satisfying aspect of fiction writing because it affords me the time to perfect every paragraph, every sentence, and every word until I become fully convinced as to the merit of my work. The editing phase can actually become almost intoxicating as I watch my story morph from an ugly caterpillar into a beautiful butterfly.

The editing phase is where I have the time to find the perfect simile without worrying about losing my train of thought. It's where I have time to find better verbs and better descriptors. It's where I have time to perform makeovers of characters I thought were interesting but who had become flat and bland. It's when I can ratchet up the level of conflict and tension and add emotion, mystery and suspense where I had neglected or under-executed those essentials in my initial draft.

This is not to say that writers should leave final editing to the very end. Far from it. I recommend that editing be done in stages, alternating between writing new chapters and editing existing chapters. What most excites you at the moment? Is there a great new scene you are dying to write, or is there an old scene you want to perfect? Let your mood be the guide. Just never intermix the two phases; never create and edit at the same time. Of course, once a final first draft is finished, the entire novel must be edited no matter how much time you have spent revising individual chapters along the way.

I do not believe there is any magical carved-in-stone process that must be followed in order to edit one's work properly. I have developed a list of tasks I recommend, but in the end, individual writers should use whatever approach they believe works best for them. Here's my editing checklist.

1. Is your main character intriguing, unique, charismatic, loveable/despicable? If you cannot honestly give an unqualified answer "yes" to this question, figure out what needs to change to make the character compelling. One of my favorite tasks during editing is to ask a lot of "What if" questions. What if Character A did such and such? What if this or that happened when he or she did so and so? You get the idea. "What if" questions often lead to new scenes and revisions that can dramatically improve the stature of a character. A little creative second-guessing about characterization can be quite productive.

2. Critically read every chapter, one at a time, and assess whether the writing adheres to the Seven Principles of Literary Excellence.

    a. Does the chapter contain adequate **literary conflict** to bring out the characters' true emotions and unique personalities?

        i. Is the main character's "want" vitally important and immediate? Are the obstacles the character faces equally monumental?

        ii. Inadequate conflict is the single most common mistake I see in manuscripts of aspiring authors. Conflict and tension that it is practically unbearable for the characters is highly entertaining to the readers.

    b. Is there enough **mystery** and **suspense**?

        i. Do you spoon-feed information slowly to the reader to keep him guessing how the conflicts you have created will be resolved?

      ii. Does the last paragraph in the chapter hook the reader and make him want to keep going?

      iii. Do you feel hooked by your story? Be fair in answering the question. If you're not excited, your readers surely will not be excited either.

c. Are the scenes depicted in the chapter **captivating**?

      i. Is the chapter a little slow to develop? Are there needless pauses in the action?

      ii. Is there unnecessary and boring chatter in the dialogue?

      iii. Is the chapter entertaining? I often buy books that have won a major book award, but quite frankly I am often disappointed. While the quality of the writing and the reflective thought these books engender are beyond question, I often find these award-winning books to be unentertaining, and toss them aside after struggling through 100 pages or so.

d. Does the dialogue portray **compelling characters** that are unique and inspiring, or is there too much sameness among the characters?

      i. Is the dialogue properly tailored to the uniqueness of each character?

      ii. Is the dialogue too formal? Too grammatically correct? Stilted, formal dialogue is unreal and must be fixed.

      iii. Does the dialogue include characterizations? "He said," is fine. "He enthusiastically said" is wrong; the dialogue itself should portray the character's enthusiasm so the writer does not have to "tell" the reader he was enthusiastic.

    e.   Do you bring out your characters' **emotions** so as to take the reader into their hearts and minds or do they float through the scenes like automatons?

3.   Back to my "What If" questions. What if some of the conflict and tension in your story addressed a current hot or controversial topic? What if your story asked some thought provoking questions about morality, religion, justice, race, national politics, or other issues in the mainstream and social media?

4.   Has the story been written to appeal to a broad audience? A few years ago, one of my students responded to a suggestion I made about improving her characterization with the comment, "Look, I'm writing this book for women; women want to read about feelings not action." I don't disagree with her statement; the characters absolutely should be appealing to women. But does that mean they cannot also be appealing to men? Do you really want to make a conscious decision to eliminate half your potential readership? That's not what most publishers are looking for.

5.   At least once during the final editing phase, the entire manuscript should be printed and the printed copy used for editing. Do not rely exclusively on the digital copy; it's never quite the same as seeing the words on paper.

6.   Have you inadvertently overused specific words, phrases, and metaphors?

7.   Is there any trite or over-flowery language?

8.   And finally, are there any typographical errors, unintentional grammatical errors, or spelling errors? Even a single stupid error is one too many.

CHAPTER 17

Publication

WHEN TO PUBLISH

D o not publish until you are really done, really satisfied, and until you have had a seasoned editor read and comment on the manuscript. There is an enormous temptation to be done, to hold a copy in your hot little hands, and to release your work to the world. This is a mistake. Readers are unforgiving when the writing appears amateurish and unprofessional. After all the hard work it takes to complete a novel, it is silly to attempt publication before your novel is the very best it can be.

PUBLISHING OPTIONS

Writers now have many options for publishing their works. Be aware, however, that the choice is often inadvertently made before the first word is written. Literary agents and major publishing houses are market driven; while quality of writing is important, the potential for large sales is far more important. In other words, if you have any ambition of selling your title through traditional sources, you should write something that will appeal to the mass markets.

I feel obligated to make this observation, because it is true, even though I totally disagree with this approach to writing. Do you enroll your child in youth sports to get a college scholarship, or do you do it to provide an enriching, enjoyable and maturing experience? Write for yourself not for the market.

1. Traditional publishing houses.

If you believe your manuscript may appeal to a large audience, either because the book itself can generate broad demand or because you have name recognition (or, as publishers call it a "platform"), go ahead and submit your book for consideration by literary agents and traditional publishers. But do so with eyes open. First, going this route will result in considerable delay in seeing your book in print. With any of the self-publishing options I mention below you will receive a printed copy in only a few months following submission; finding a traditional publisher will likely take a year or two, and even then you may well have nothing to show for your efforts. Second, be prepared for rejection. My novel was rejected at least 250 times before I found a publisher who offered to take it on.

Finally, all publishers want their authors to play a major role in selling their books. They want you to maintain websites, publish regular blogs, build a major following through Facebook and Twitter, attend writers' conferences and shows, organize book signings, and work hard to promote the book. Publishers help, but they all see their writers as partners willing to invest substantial time and, oftentimes, some of their own money. If you're not ready for that, self-publishing may be a better route for you because then you can do as much or as little as you like.

Unless you know, or can obtain an introduction to, someone in a given publishing house, or unless there is a publisher with a known market niche that perfectly fits the audience for your book, you are best advised to try first to search for a literary agent. Manuscripts sent unsolicited to most publishers almost invariably have a bleak future.

There are hundreds of literary agents in the United States. Most work on commission, but a few are fee-for-service. I do not recommend fee-for-service agents because they have zero incentive to sell the book. They get paid the same either way. Most literary agents specialize in certain categories or genres, and it is wise to research the field before sending off any query letters or manuscripts.

There are many on-line resources that provide listings of literary agents and their interests. I provide a partial listing below, but you will find additional resources with a bit of research on the internet. Most literary agencies have special requirements that you must follow; in fact, each agent in a given agency may have different submission requirements. Some want only a brief query letter. Others accept a query letter and, for instance, one chapter. Some want only e-mail or on-line submissions while others insist on hard copies. Virtually all agencies that accept hard copies want SASE (self-addressed, stamped envelope) for return of your submission and their response to your query. Follow all individual instructions precisely, or your query is likely to be ignored.

Learn how to write query letters. It is easy to find several helpful articles on the internet, but, in addition, you should pay close attention to the websites of each literary agency you consider. Often these agencies and their individual agents give clues as to what they are looking for, and it helps to tailor your standard form query letter to their apparent interests and biases.

Literary Agents – Partial List of On-Line Resources

- PW.org (Poets and Writers), maintains a list of subscribing literary agents with filters to allow you to select those with a stated interest in a given genre.
- PublishersMarketplace.com. A one-month subscription is required to access its extensive data base of agents.

- AgentQuery.com maintains a database of literary agents and an on-line chat room.
- QueryTracker.net has a searchable database of literary agents.
- Jeff Herman's Guide to Book Publishers, Editors, and Literary Agents.

2. Publishing Services Companies.

There are a number of companies who provide a la carte publishing services for a fee. All require that submitted manuscripts be reasonably well written and inoffensive, but their standards are generally easy to meet. These companies will design a cover, format the book properly, provide editing services, obtain the ISBN number, obtain copyrights, print whatever number of copies you want, provide print-on-demand capabilities, and provide advice about promoting the book. They will distribute both print copies and e-editions through all normal retail and on-line outlets. In essence they will do everything a traditional publishing house will do, but you pay for whichever services you select. Prices vary from roughly $2,000 to $20,000 depending on the options you designate.

Publishing services companies are easy to find on the internet. I list a few of them below, but I encourage you to do your own research as every vendor has slightly different service offerings and price structures.

- Archway Publishing. Subsidiary of Simon and Schuster but managed independently. It provides a full a la carte package of services ranging from $2,000 to $14,000. Archway is well managed, very professional, and adheres to the strict standards set by Simon and Schuster.
- Austin Macauley Publishers www.austinmacauley.com It publishes books, eBooks and audiobooks. The home office

is in London, but it has a branch office in New York. It accepts full, unsolicited manuscripts and either agrees to publish them traditionally or provide a publishing fee-for-services contract.

- Dorrance Publishing Company. Provides full service coaching, editing, publishing and promotion services. Dorrance is probably the oldest and best-known company in the publishing services business.

3. Pure self-publishing (sometimes impolitely characterized as "vanity press")

The companies listed below publish exactly what you send them, good or bad. A few offer limited services for a fee, while others simply allow you to download whatever you want, and they will print on demand any orders they receive. Some do both print and e-copies; others do only e-copies.

- BookBaby. Print on demand services, provides some help with formatting, design, distribution.
- CreateSpace. A division of Amazon, no upfront cost, no professional services, such as editing, interior or cover design, or conversion to eBooks.
- Draft2Digital. No upfront fee, minimal support with format, design and distribution.
- IngramSpark (www.ingramspark.com) Worldwide distribution, print or digital. Staff will help uploading book in correct format; gets access to Amazon, Barnes and Noble and dozens of other retailers of paper and digital books. Fee for service.
- Smashwords E-book publishing only, distributes to all major retailers except Amazon, no upfront fee.
- A good resource is Jane Friedman's book: *How to Self-Publish Your Book*

PROMOTION

Books will not sell if they are not promoted. Even once a book finds its way onto a bookstore shelf, it will not sell unless it is promoted, and if it does not sell, the bookstores will quickly return them. Before you incur expense in self-publishing your book, it is wise to have a plan for promoting it. Otherwise, once you have exhausted your supply of family and friends, sales will quickly dwindle. Professional publicists are available to assist in promoting your book, but they are expensive, so most self-published authors also self-promote their books. Here are some options.

1. Develop a mail and e-mail list of everyone you know and invite everyone to at least two book signings or readings.
2. Print a simple business card using the cover of your book on one side and your contact information and links to websites where the book may be obtained on the other side. Carry a stack of these wherever you go so that when the subject of your novel arises, you can hand everyone a card informing them how to buy it.
3. Go to all local writers' shows and conferences.
4. Ask all your friends whether they are in book clubs and, if so, if you can come and read from your book, or, better yet, discuss your book after club members have read it.
5. Submit your book for literary competitions in the year of publication.
6. Schedule book signings at bookstores, clubs, shows, etc. Invitations to book signings should be personalized so recipients do not think the invitation is junk mail.
7. Speak at any gathering you can get yourself invited to attend. Many organizations are constantly looking for free speakers, and published authors are often quite welcome.
8. Submit your book for reviews by all print media.
9. Set up a website.

10. Set up a regular blog.
11. Purchase Google ad words.
12. Ask everyone who says they like your book to write a review on Amazon. Frequent reviews and sales keep your book on Amazon's first page of like searches.

CHAPTER 1

In less than one page, write an outline for a plot that contains intense conflict and a compelling character.

A possible response

In 1990, Enrique Gomez was brought illegally to California by his mother. He was less than a year old at the time. He has never returned to Mexico and does not speak a word of Spanish. He has pulled himself up by his bootstraps and has recently become a licensed medical doctor who runs a small clinic, funded mostly by charity and devoted to providing quality medical care to poor and homeless people. When he is stopped by police for having a broken taillight on his car, his illegal immigration status is uncovered and he is arrested and jailed. ICE demands that the local police turn him over so it can deport him to Mexico. That's the real beginning of a story that focuses on the vagaries and injustice of an American immigration system that would expel such an outstanding contributor to American life as Dr. Gomez. Here's the conflict that makes Dr. Gomez so compelling.

- The police chief refuses to turn Gomez over to ICE because the San Diego city council voted to declare the city an Immigration Sanctuary City. Instead, the chief takes protective custody of Gomez and houses him in a private room at the city government center. ICE in turn files suit against the police chief in U.S. District Court.

- The State of California and Gomez file suit against the President in a different federal court.
- The ACLU takes an interest in the case; so does the Justice Department – on opposite sides.
- One California Senator strongly supports his cause; the other opposes it – both of them to satisfy their perceived political base.
- The U.S. President rejects pardoning Gomez and orders ICE to deport him forthwith for violation of immigration laws.
- Congress stalls on addressing immigration reform legislation over the President's demand to add money for a wall to any reform legislation.
- Gomez' wife, a legal resident, delivers their first child while he is in custody. Although Gomez is legally free to leave protective custody to see his new child he choses to stay put because of fear that ICE will find him and promptly deport him.
- Multiple court hearings before multiple judges fail to resolve the issue.
- A patient from Gomez' clinic dies from complications of diabetes because, without Dr. Gomez, she could not renew her vital prescriptions.
- San Diego's mayor leads an effort to relocate Gomez' medical clinic to the grounds of the San Diego government center and moves a city office out of the building to create a space for the clinic. Gomez begins seeing his old patients inside the jail.
- A right wing group begins an attack campaign against the mayor.

- The President orders ICE to invade City Hall to arrest Gomez, but the Governor of California orders the state National Guard to deny entry to ICE.
- The local and national news media become involved and create quite a media circus surrounding the affair.
- Social media goes viral, with vitriolic hotheads on both sides of the issue.
- The State of California adopts its own immigration laws applicable to all persons residing in California. It specifically grants California citizenship to all Dreamers.
- Arizona retaliates and adopts legislation requiring all state police and the Arizona National Guard to seek out and arrest all illegal immigrants.
- Still Congress does nothing.
- Still Gomez lingers in protective custody.

Does this story satisfy my principle of intense literary conflict? It's your call, but here's my take. First, conflict is rampant: ICE versus Gomez; one senator versus another; one court versus another; California versus the President; the ACLU versus the Justice Department; the mayor and chief of police versus right wing groups; and justice versus political expediency. Second, Dr. Gomez has the potential to become a highly compelling character. He is the epitome of the highly deserving underdog in a desperate fight for his family and his patients against an enormously powerful enemy, the United States Government.

CHAPTER 2

Write a brief scene, using either narrative or dialogue, which portrays a compelling character. The scene must contain conflict, emotion, and artistic vision.

Possible Response

"The choice is yours, Nolan," Charles Hawking said.

Nolan Childs, first year associate at the New York mega law firm of Hart and McDowell, did not move a muscle. He stared past the intense eyes of the senior partner at the original Picasso hanging unpretentiously on the wall behind his hand-carved mahogany desk. The insides of his skull whirred like a super computer. All that he'd worked for, all his years of sacrifice to reach the very chair that he now occupied, all of it depended on the next few words he would utter.

"All we expect of our young recruits," Hawking continued, "is loyalty and commitment. That's why you've got a salary of $180,000 when the rest of the dime-a-dozen lawyers in your law school class are driving 8-year old cars."

Maybe it isn't that bad, Childs thought to himself, his mind wandering off to the new yellow Porsche in the parking stall 75 stories below. But he also thought of his wife, now 8 months pregnant, and the huge mortgage they recently took out on their west side condominium. One document, that's all, no big deal. He tried to force eye contact with Hawking, but his ocular muscles would not cooperate.

"Without loyalty, Nolan, there can be no trust," Hawking said in a quiet and controlled voice. "And a legal partnership is built on trust. But, of course the valedictorian of the Yale Law School class of 2017 undoubtedly appreciates the need for trust at Hart and McDowell."

A few seconds seemed like hours, and Childs shifted uneasily in his chair.

"You know," Hawking said, "some of my partners were a little nervous about bringing you into the firm. I pushed hard for you because, quite frankly, I have exactly the kind of complete trust in you that we expect you to have for us."

Childs forced his eyes to focus on Hawking, but he would not allow his facial expression to reveal his confused thoughts.

"Any way," Hawking said, "a couple of the guys have built a little file on you. It's not exactly the kind of file you'd want any future potential employer to read."

Childs rose from his leather chair at the front of Hawking's desk, managed a twinge of a smile to cross his lips, and strode silently out of the room.

What's your verdict? Is Childs a compelling character? Childs has been forced into making an untenable choice: to save his legal career by violating his oath as an attorney and committing an unethical act or to throw a potentially great legal career to the wind and force his family to endure severe economic hardship. This is precisely the type of literary conflict from which compelling characters are born. And Childs is made all the more compelling because he never spoke a single word during the meeting. He didn't need to speak; he needed to act.

But how about Hawking? Is he a compelling character? Evil doers can be as compelling as do gooders, and Hawking, by forcing such an unjust and harsh choice on his associate certainly qualifies as an evil doer. So, it's good versus evil, exactly what readers want to see. The scene has given readers one character to cheer on as the story progresses and another at whom to boo and hiss. There's a lot more story to be told, to be sure, but this is a nice start at creating two characters who will fight an epic battle over good versus evil as the story unfolds.

CHAPTER 3

Identify any human emotion and then write a brief scene, using either narrative or dialogue, in order to fully capture that emotion. The scene itself must depict the emotion, and you may not either identify the emotion specifically or use any word synonymous with the emotion in writing the scene. The goal is that any person reading the scene for the first time will immediately be able to identify the emotion you have selected.

Possible response

The Emotion to be Depicted: Love

Anton took Elena's hand and fingered the small diamond he'd given her only the week before. It had shifted off to one side and he carefully re-centered it on her finger. "Are you embarrassed to show off your ring?" he asked.

She smiled and twisted the diamond fully out of view under her hand. "Maybe I won't wear it at all while you're at sea," she whispered into his ear as she simultaneously caressed the side of his cheek.

He pulled her closer and wrapped his arms around her, engulfing her and her favorite pink sweater. "Do what you will with the ring; I got my gloms on your heart and I will surely never let it go."

She squeezed him back. She wanted to speak, tell him her feelings, but the words would not come.

He put his finger to her lips. "Words are all so meaningless today," he said, pulling her as close to him as physics would allow, full of emotions that their hugs proclaimed would last a lifetime.

"Good-bye," he said finally, releasing her from his embrace.

She could not voice those words in return. She watched him

disappear into a crowd of men, laughing and talking young men in uniform, one of them taking with him the heart of the girl in the pink sweater.

This passage, although teetering uneasily at the brink of schmaltziness, illustrates a simple example of using mostly dialogue to paint a very emotional scene, in this case a scene of the fresh but naïve young love of a departing sailor.

CHAPTER 4

Write a short plotline for a captivating story. The plotline should demonstrate that the story is entertaining, imaginative, amazing, suspenseful, and reflective.

Possible Response

I propose a story about the enormous struggles of a Somali family, recently immigrated to Minnesota on a political asylum visa. The family of four are devote Muslims and have fled Somalia because Abdul's life was threatened by al-Shabaab rebels. The family has very strong bonds to each other, and they are all bright, kind, motivated, and honest people whose only want is to find safety and happiness in Minnesota. Their obstacles are many:

- None of the family speaks English when they arrive in Minnesota.
- While Abdul is very bright, he has no employable skills on arrival.
- Their only friends in Minneapolis are cousins who have failed to acclimate themselves to American customs and who offer poor advice about becoming established in America.
- Abdul gets work as an unskilled laborer but is quickly fired because of his insistence on observing Muslim afternoon prayers during the workday.
- Abdul's wife, Aadila, is severely injured when she is punched in the face with a beer bottle for refusing to remove her headscarf while seated in a restaurant with her children.
- Abdul's son, Muhammad, is bullied at school for being skinny and non-athletic.

- Muhammad is later arrested for loaning money to his cousin who attempted to use the money to buy airfare to Syria to join ISIS.
- Abdul's daughter, Aafa, is bullied at school for wearing a burka and refusing to join any school activities where burkas are an inconvenience.
- The family feels threatened when their white school principal comes to their home to help the family adapt and assimilate. The principal in turn feels rejected and frustrated.
- Help finally comes when, after airing of a newscast featuring the racially motivated assault on Aadila, there is an enormous outpouring of public support for the family. But it is a long struggle, learning English, adapting to American ways, learning a trade, obtaining employment, finding a stable network of friends, and until the very end, it is unclear whether they will succeed or fail.

A major goal of the plotline is to outline the conflicts that will guide the story. At this stage there is no need to provide a lot of detail; detail follows naturally once the obstacles the writer intends to foist onto his main characters are identified. Do you think this story has the potential to captivate interested readers? Do you think this story has the potential to be entertaining, imaginative, amazing, and suspenseful? Do you think it has the possibility to stimulate reflective thought about the assimilation of other cultures into American society? If your vote is "No," what needs to happen for you to change your mind?

CHAPTER 5

Write the first and last sentences of the first chapter of a novel of any genre of your choosing. The goal is to use mystery and suspense to hook the reader into the story after only one sentence and to keep the reader aroused so he will immediately want to read the second chapter.

First sentence of a murder mystery

As nighttime suffocated the last feeble rays of a December sun and the first of the cold winter winds battered the ancient timbers of the old prairie church I had served for nearly two decades, little did I know that the furious winter that was about to begin would see three men and a child die in this peaceful, sacred place.

Last sentence of first chapter of the same murder mystery

"It's so good to see you here every Sunday morning, Ollie," Pastor Mitchell said as he greeted departing parishioners at the foyer, "must be 30 years or better by now."

"39," Ollie replied.

Pastor Mitchell took Ollie's hand and shook it warmly. "You're a real inspiration to the entire community," he said, "thank you."

"May not feel that way much longer," Ollie said as he pulled his hand away and ambled down the church steps towards his old red pickup.

Success or failure; you be the judge. Would you buy this book if these were the only sentences you read before deciding (assuming of course that you are looking for a good mystery)? Did these few lines get you hooked? Did the first paragraph excite your curiosity and draw you into the story? If your vote is "No," what needs to happen for you to feel differently? How about the last paragraph – does that entice you to read on?

I attempted to accomplish these goals by introducing mystery immediately, both in the first paragraph and in the last sentence of the chapter. Why would Ollie, a loyal parishioner for 39 years drop the warm handshake of Pastor Mitchell? Why would he elude to the possibility that he might be involved in something sinister? Will he be the murderer suggested in the first paragraph? Probably not, writers do not solve their mysteries in the first chapter; so what is really going on with him?

It's too early to say whether either Pastor Mitchell or Ollie will become compelling characters, but the possibility clearly exists. Just being the long-time pastor of a very small church where three murders occur is a good first stab at turning Pastor Mitchell into a compelling figure. Ollie likewise has possibilities with his mysterious behavior towards his long-time pastor. Are Ollie and Pastor Mitchell totally normal people, or do you expect that they will transcend the South Dakota prairie to become people you want to read about? If you say "No," how would you change the story to accomplish the assignment?

CHAPTER 6

Select either of the pictures contained in this chapter and write no more than one page, using either narrative or dialogue, to capture your interpretation of the picture. Let your vision and imagination roam wild.

Possible Response re the white clapboard church on the prairie

For almost a half century the Reverend Nathaniel Mitchell ministered kindness and compassion from that old clapboard church on the prairie, and in return, for one hour every week, virtually every farm family in the county filled the lovely old structure with song and celebration of the Word of the Lord.

He just showed up one day, all by himself. Just walked into town and never left. I still don't know where he came from or how he got there, 'cepting it was on foot. No point in asking, didn't really matter anyway.

He told me later, just before he died, that he admired the tidiness of all the nearby farmsteads. Figured they belonged to God-fearing people, I guess, though he never exactly said that. Told folks at the Prairie Ridge Café that he was a preacher. Said he was gonna build a church for himself. Some folks thought it a bit strange, just showing up and building a church. Had nothing but what he was wearing, plus a small leather satchel. That was it. Didn't seem to be wanting for nothing though. Pleasant fellow, I thought. And he never proved me wrong.

"Heard you were looking for a place for a church," I asked him a few days later.

"I recon a town like this'd do well with a little religion once in a spell."

"Where you thinkin' a church might go?" I asked.

"Be nice in town, but it'd work anywhere 'round here if I could find myself a small spot of land."

That was that. I gave him a corner out of one of my sections. He built the little church with his own hand. Two years he spent pounding nails. That was 50 years ago and it's still there doing its job.

My assignment in this drill was to paint a picture of this lovely rural church, and I chose to do so through the actions of its preacher. Notice that I barely mention the building itself and never describe it, but that the scene nevertheless captures the spirit of the building in a way that a verbal description could never accomplish. The drill is not about showing versus telling, although this scene certainly meets that requirement. The drill is instead about artistic vision, painting a picture of the church from inside out, that is, a picture that invites the reader inside with the preacher and all his parishioners. The test of my success or failure on this drill is whether the reader of the scene can picture himself sitting in a back pew on a Sunday morning fully immersed in the life of the little church on the prairie. Did I pass the test? If not, how would you rewrite the passage to make it better?

CHAPTER 7

Write a short sentence that "tells" any fact you wish. (Examples: I saw a powerful tornado quickly approaching my farmhouse; Sarah was a beautiful woman, perfect complexion, gorgeous blond hair and a perfect hourglass figure; Zack was an evil man through and through.) Pick any subject you wish. Then write no more than one paragraph that "shows" what you "told."

Possible Response: "I saw a powerful tornado quickly approaching my farmhouse."

As I sowed the last row of corn on what had been a beautiful spring day, an enormous black cloud suddenly appeared on the horizon and snuffed out the sun as if it were but a small votive. In seconds day became night. My old clapboard farmhouse at the edge of the field was the last to lose its serene springtime glow, morphing spontaneously into the vast blackness that now overran my tractor. The black monster roared across the field and with a mammoth arm grabbed at everything in its path and tore it to shreds. I leapt into a culvert at the edge of the field and in an instant watched my tractor lofted into the darkness. I closed my eyes and prayed.

This may be a bit too much metaphor and simile for describing a scene that probably plays only a very small role in the storyline, but it is useful nonetheless for making my point about showing versus telling. The assignment in the drill was to describe a fast-moving and powerful tornado without using the words "powerful," or "tornado," or any synonymous words, in the description. That is, my goal was to "show" a powerful tornado. Mission accomplished. Any reasonable reader will easily be able to picture an image of a fast and powerful tornado that is on the verge of destroying the farmhouse.

INDEX

Printed in the United States
By Bookmasters